VARIETIES OF PRESENCE

VARIETIES OF PRESENCE

ALVA NOË

HARVARD UNIVERSITY PRESS
Cambridge, Massachusetts
London, England
2012

Library of Congress Cataloging-in-Publication Data

Noë, Alva.
Varieties of presence / Alva Noë.
p. cm.
Includes bibliographical references (p.) and index.
ISBN 978-0-674-06214-6 (alk. paper)
1. Experience.   I. Title.
B105.E9N64 2012
128'.4—dc23   2011040580

For Hilary Putnam

"The world is all that is the case."

Contents

Preface

THE WORLD shows up for us, in thought, and in experience; the world is present to mind. This phenomenon—presence—is the basic phenomenon in the whole domain of the mental. It is what is at stake in disputes over the nature of "intentionality," and it is the heart of the problem of consciousness.

In this book I investigate the phenomenon of presence. My main idea is that presence is achieved, and that its varieties correspond to the variety of ways we skillfully achieve access to the world.

Varieties of Presence consists of seven chapters (and also an introduction, afterword, and appendix) each of which was written as a self-standing essay between 2003 and 2011, after I had joined the philosophy faculty at University of California, Berkeley, and after I had finished *Action in Perception* (which was published at the end of 2004). I have reframed many of these essays in light of the vantage point I now enjoy. Although each chapter can be read on its own, the book is not merely a collection of essays; it is an integrated investigation of its topic.

I have written *Varieties of Presence* in the context of intellectual exchange with colleagues and students in Berkeley. The chapters are in some ways adaptations to their criticism. Throughout I have tried to make myself intelligible to them. I have in mind in particular John Campbell, Hubert Dreyfus, Kristina Gehrman, James Genone, Hanna Ginsborg, Mike Martin, and James Stazicker. I am enormously grateful to these teachers, students, and friends. More recently, I have benefited from the insightful criticism of Caitlin Dolan and Martin Weichold.

The appendix has a different sort of origin. In the summer of 2010, dancer and choreographer Nicole Peisl and I created and presented a work of performance entitled *What We Know Best*. The work was produced in the context of a dance festival called Sommerlabor at Künstlerhaus, Mousonturm, in Frankfurt, Germany. The aim of *What We Know Best* was, among other things, to investigate what it is to introduce oneself to others, to show oneself, to make oneself *present*, on the stage, and for another. The text of the appendix is taken from this joint work.

In March 2011 I presented a version of *Varieties of Presence* to the members of the Collegium for Advanced Study of Picture Act and Embodiment at the Humboldt University, Berlin, where I am a fellow. I am grateful for the vigorous and productive criticism that I received from Horst Bredekamp, Alex Arteaga, Rebekka Hufendiek, and Joerg Fingerhut, as well as from others.

Many writers and friends have inspired me and in different ways provoked me, although not always through any direct communication. I would like to mention Stanley Cavell, Jim Conant, Scott DeLahunta, Bill Forsythe, Warren Goldfarb, Blake Gopnik, Edward Harcourt, John McDowell, Alex Nagel, Nicole Peisl, Evan Thompson, and Dan Zahavi.

I have a special debt to Susan Hurley, with whom I worked closely on the nature of consciousness and the philosophy of neuroscience while I was at work on the material that comprises this book. *Out of Our Heads: Why You Are Not Your Brain and Other Lessons from the Biology of Consciousness,* which I planned before Susan's death, but wrote in the eighteen months immediately thereafter, registers some of the fruits of our joint work.

I thank Lindsay Waters of Harvard University Press for his support for this project and Mateo Duque for his work preparing the index.

I dedicate this book to Hilary Putnam; he is my model of brilliance and grace.

VARIETIES OF PRESENCE

Introduction: Free Presence

I BEGIN with an everyday experience. You go to an art gallery and you look at a work of art in an unfamiliar style by an artist you don't know. It happens, sometimes, in a situation like this, that the work of art strikes you as flat or opaque. You don't get it. It is incomprehensible.

But you don't give up. You look harder; maybe you recall another similar object that you've seen. You read the title of the piece and that gives you an idea. You overhear someone in the gallery make a comment about the piece—about how it was made. Or perhaps you are with a friend and you talk with each other about what is there in the work.

Something remarkable can now occur. The piece opens up to you; it discloses its face to you; you can see into it now and appreciate its structure. The piece now is present to you as meaningful.

There are two points to be made about this phenomenon. First, although your experience of the art work has been transformed, there is no change in the work itself. It has no more (or less) structure or meaning now than it did at the outset. So if there is a change, a transformation, it is a transformation in you, or perhaps, in your situation.

Second, whatever change it is that is brought about in you, it is not a merely subjective change. It is not as if what has happened is that you now feel differently about what you see, or have different beliefs about it. Whatever change has occurred, it enables you now to perceive, in the work, what you couldn't perceive before.

There is a name for the transformation in you that makes it possible for you first to perceive what is there before you; it is called understanding.

The work of art becomes visible through the understanding. Understanding enables us to perceive, factively, in the work, what we could not perceive before.

My subject matter in this book is not art, but experience and thought in general, and the central role understanding, knowledge and skill play in opening up the world for experience. What is true of the experience of the work of art is true of human experience quite generally. The world shows up for us in experience only insofar as we know how to make contact with it, or, to use a different metaphor, only insofar as we are able to bring it into focus. One reason why art is so important to us is that it recapitulates this fundamental fact about our relation to the world around us: the world is blank and flat until we understand it.[1]

The world shows up for us. But it doesn't show up for free. This is my main focus in this book. We achieve access to the world around us through skillful engagement; we acquire and deploy the skills needed to bring the world into focus.

Presence is manifestly fragile. This idea will be developed throughout; it is a discovery. We spontaneously squint our eyes and shift our head and body position to keep things in view, or to get a better look at things that interest us. In this way we exhibit our sensitivity to the fragility of our access to the world. Wittgenstein entertained the thought, in the *Tractatus*, that the eyeball is the limit of the visual field, the point from which the field is presented.[2] But that's wrong. The "visual field," in this sense of Wittgenstein, may have something to do with geometry and artificial perspective, but nothing whatsoever to do with experience. True, we don't see the eye with the eye (unless we look in a mirror). But our perceptual relation to the world around us is more like that of an outfielder shagging fly balls. We ourselves—eyes, bodies, feet and all—are at work in the field of play. And this is *manifestly* so, that is, it is reflected in the very manner in which anything ever shows up in

---

1. I often use the material presented in these opening paragraphs in lectures as a way of introducing and elucidating the phenomenon. The text here is adapted from one such lecture, given in Berlin in April 2006 and eventually published as "Making Worlds Available" (Noë 2007). I use the text here with permission. Thanks to Alex Arteaga and Rebekka Hufendiek for useful comments on these passages.
2. See Wittgenstein's *Tractatus Logico-Philosophicus* (1922, 5.633, 5.6331).

experience. The world does not show up as presented on a viewing screen; it shows up as the situation in which we find ourselves.

The same point can be appreciated in relation to questions about meaning and grammar. The question what a word or phrase means is one we pose *within* language. The meaning-question—what does this mean?—is one of language's affordances; it is an opportunity that is always just around the corner. We don't just *use* words, we criticize and reflect on the use of words, we query and ponder meaning. Or rather, criticism, reflection and refinement belong to the unproblematic language-internal ways we use words. We don't settle questions of meaning (or grammar) at the limits of language, as it were drawing the limits by tying language to the world. We don't ever get to the limits of language.

One way to make this point is that when it comes to language and meaning, we can't make a clean distinction between the first-order linguistic practice and the second-order practice of thinking about our linguistic behavior. The first-order practice contains within it the second-order practice. For thinking about language and language-use is one of the basic and unavoidable things we use language to do. There is no such thing as the naïve, unreflective, theoretically unbiased user of language. For to understand a word is to know how to use it, and that means, among other things, knowing how to explain its use to another, how to answer the question *what does this mean?* And also how to criticize or correct the usage of others as well as to defend or justify one's own usage. To be a language-user is perforce to be a critic. And the job of criticism is not to criticize language from without—as if there were practice-neutral rules and regulations—but rather to enact, or maybe just to recommend, ways of carrying on within the practice.

Questions of meaning and presence are, in a basic sense, questions of style. We do things with style. That is, there are distinctive ways we achieve access to the world around us, and to these different styles or manners of carrying on there correspond different ways in which worlds (words, meanings, pictures, people, places, problems, everything) can show up for us. Style, and its basic importance for us, is an additional preoccupation of this book.

To acknowledge that presence is achieved and that it is achieved in full understanding of its manifest fragility is really to give up the idea that the world shows up as a remote object of contemplation. Perception is a transaction; it is the sharing of a situation with what you perceive.

And something similar is true of thought. To think of something is to be in a causal-conceptual space that contains both you and that of which you think. Our attitude to the world is not that of the voyeur. Nor is it primarily, or usually, intellectual, which is not to say that it is divorced from understanding, knowledge, or the intellect. We look at the world, yes, but the world looks back! We are always in the midst of making adjustments to the world around us. And we are always liable to be caught in the act!

Much traditional thought about perception takes shape from the question: how do we get from *in here* (these images, these sensations, these sense data) to the world *out there*. Like many contemporary thinkers, I try to find an alternative way of understanding the perceptual predicament in which we find ourselves.

The traditional view is misguided not only in the way it presents us as in experience cut off from the world, as confined, e.g., to mere sensation or appearance. The traditional view is misguided further in its conception of what it would be for us to achieve contact with the world. Authentic perceptual awareness, according to this conception, would be, *per impossibile*, an awareness of objects that was, in its epistemological character, exactly like what the awareness of sense data is supposed to be: it would be immediate and infallible.

But the traditional view gets something right; it isn't hard to see why we find it so difficult to shake off its hold on our theoretical imagination.

What the traditional view gets right is that perception is a direct encounter; nothing could count as an episode of perceptual consciousness if it could happen in isolation from its apparent objects. It gets wrong the idea that only sense data and other "private" contents of consciousness can satisfy this stringent condition of being objects of awareness.

The tradition also gets right that our encounters with situations and things are, in a certain sense, always only partial and incomplete. For we only ever encounter situations and things in a limited way—from this distance, with all that noise, despite those obstacles, and so on. Every perceptual experience is always, at best, a work in progress.

Where the tradition again goes wrong, however, is in its insistence that this entails we are confined to the *interior* contents of consciousness (sense data). The agent with the right kind of skills and equipment—

mobility of eyes and head, the ability to read, etc.—engages the world itself.

Instead of thinking of perception as a passage from inside to outside, from in here to out there, I urge, in this book, that we think of perception as a movement from here to there, from this place to that. We ourselves (whole persons) undertake our perceptual consciousness of the world in, with, and in relation to the places where we find ourselves. We are at home in the world.

To resist traditional approaches to presence—this should be clear—is to resist different ways of denying presence.

It may help to consider two different ways of thinking about *theater.* In one way, audience and performers are together; they share a space and they are both present to each other. This is the sort of shared, real presence we enjoy today at sporting events. We are there to be eyewitnesses to the spectacle.

In a second, distinctively modern way of understanding theater, actors no longer share a space with an audience; they reside in a symbolic space.[3] They might as well be projections on a movie screen. We read them, or interpret them, or try to understand the story. We don't *witness* anything.

Modern theater denies real presence. But we might just as well say that the standpoint of modern *science* treats all presence as merely, in this new way, theatrical.

Modern science teaches, supposedly, that there is only matter. So everything else—the different kinds of things that there are such as people or microbes or poems or orgasms or wars or gods or feelings or art—can only be matter redescribed or reinterpreted. The world shows up for us as it does because we project or interpret or confabulate or hypothesize. From this standpoint, presence can be at best only symbolic, and we human beings have our assigned role as representers or symbolizers. We stand above or apart, detached; we make up meaning; we posit and we hypothesize, in something like the way a scientist might posit the existence of an unobserved force, or in the way that a reader interprets the

---

3. Here, and in these next paragraphs, I touch on themes that are developed beautifully in Hans Ulrich Gumbrecht's *The Production of Presence* (2004).

upshot of a story, but also in something like the way a mad person makes up stories with no foundation in reality. And this conception of ourselves requires that, if we wish to understand the nature of our human experience, really, we need to turn our attention inward, to the mind (or the brain!), for that is where we, our individual selves, stage reality.

I said before that we never bear witness in the modern theater. We are like readers or researchers, not like bystanders. There is, however, one striking exception to this rule. When something goes wrong and the stagecraft comes undone. Then, as if by magic, or rather, as if thanks to the disruption of magic, everything changes, the house lights go up, and we find ourselves transformed. We are embarrassed!

This embarrassment is interesting. We don't experience it when the team loses, or the trapeze artist falls. We experience it rather when a line is forgotten, or, perhaps, when a scene stretches out to the point of boredom. Embarrassment is a giveaway not of our sympathy but of our complicity; the embarrassment tells that the theatrical denial of real presence was always really just a pretense. We had been averting our gaze the whole time, pretending not to notice the actors' makeup, or our own forbidden desire to get up and visit the toilets.

And our vulnerability to this embarrassment—and not only in the theater!—is important. It is a symptom of our modernity. Take the case of the Catholic sacrament of the Eucharist. Does the wine symbolize blood? Or is it blood? Are you believers? Or are you actors? There is always leakage between these different stances. Or to return to the theatrical example: the possibility of something going wrong on stage is always a live one; as audience, we only pretend that we are not alert to it. Like listening to LP records in a house with small children—you're just waiting for that leap from the couch that will make the record skip!

Our liability to embarrassment is not only a symptom of our modernity, it is evidence of modernity's only fragile hold on us. You are not your brain. And your friend is not a construct inside you. She is not a representation in your mind, and her thoughts and feelings are not hidden inside *her* head. Your consciousness of her and the larger world around you is not an intellectual feat. The world is not a projection on a movie screen.

Existential phenomenologists, such as Heidegger, Merleau-Ponty and Dreyfus—I think we can place Derrida in this list as well, although I won't try to discuss him here—have found a different, but no less troubling way of denying presence. These writers discern problems with the modern way of thinking about presence, but because, as it seems to me, they can imagine no alternative way of grasping the phenomenon, they jettison the very idea of presence. What they really discover are new ways of thinking about presence, not alternatives to it. They discover the varieties of presence.

For existential phenomenology what is basic in human experience is not our capacity for thoughtful observation or understanding of the world where we find ourselves, but rather, the fact of our unthinking attunement. This attunement takes the form of a readiness to act, and of the disappearance both of the need for and also the possibility of looking and finding out how things are. The world does not really *show up* for us at all; for Heidegger, rather, it "withdraws," at least when we are engaged and at home in it. The world is unobtrusive and unthought. If my book were written by existential phenomenologists, it would have been entitled not *Varieties of Presence,* but rather *Varieties of Absence.* Heidegger explains:

> "Unthought" means that it [roughly, the scene around us] is not thematically apprehended for deliberate thinking about things; instead, in circumspection, we find our bearings in regard to them ... When we enter here through the door, we do not apprehend the seats, and the same holds for the doorknob. (1972/1988, 163)[4]

For Heidegger we live for the most part not in a world of objects and properties. What is "given" to us is

> the "for writing," the "for going in and out," ... "for sitting." That is, writing, going-in-and-out, sitting, and the like are that wherein we a priori move. What we know when we "know our way around." (Heidegger 1975/1982, 144)[5]

For Heidegger, this sort of unthought, unmediated, unthematized readiness-to-hand stands in sharp contrast to presence. Presence, for Heidegger, is always the representation of a feature or object in thought or experience, and so it is always correlated with observation, or

---

4. This text is based on lectures given in Marburg in 1927.
5. Translated by Herbert Dreyfus. Used with his permission.

contemplation. Talk of presence, for Heidegger, is always talk of a kind of thought-mediated intellectual detachment from the world around us. And so the contrast with readiness-to-hand could not be plainer. Take an example: A baseball player uses his glove to field a ground ball; he relies on his glove, uses it, acts with and through it; the glove is not an object he perceives and evaluates; he does not represent it. It is equipment (*Zeug*, in German); it is like the ground he stands on. Or it is an extension of himself, something with which he has merged.

Heidegger's discovery of the distinct place of equipment in our lives, and his elaboration, more generally, of the way the world's furniture and stuff can withdraw and absent themselves, cannot be gainsayed. It is a marvelous and beautiful philosophical achievement. But he makes two critical errors, I believe, and these blind him to the fact that his real discovery is not that absence, as opposed to presence, is what is basic in our lives. He identifies and understands a variety of presence that, for many reasons, modern philosophy has failed to understand.

A remark of Hubert Dreyfus can help bring this into focus.[6] Dreyfus writes:

> According to the existential phenomenologists, the transcendental account is not wrong but it is secondary. The phenomenologists claim that the absorption into the field of attractions and repulsions they have brought to light is a primordial nonconceptual mode of coping *on the basis of which* the conceptual world makes sense. (2012, in press)

But this is exactly wrong. What Dreyfus here calls the transcendental account—the modern view that existential phenomenology opposes viz. that we are intellectual interpreters whose basic relation to the world around us is that of detached representer and interpreter—is wrong *even as an account of thought*. Such a conception of the intellect—as a modality of detachment rather than a modality of openness to the world, to use McDowell's (1994) phrase—violently distorts our lives as

---

6. (Dreyfus 2011). This paper is Dreyfus's final contribution to an extended exchange with John McDowell. Dreyfus characterizes McDowell's view as "a transcendentalist account." I intervene in this debate here in this introduction, but also elsewhere in this book (see especially Chapters 6 and 7), and also in Noë (2004, Chapter 6). For the debate itself, see Dreyfus (2006; 2012), as well as McDowell (2007a; 2007b). See also Joseph Schear's collection (2012) for a collection of writings devoted to this topic.

thinkers, perceivers, and doers. If thought is always explicit, deliberate, detached, cut off, broken down, disengaged, then of course it must seem compulsory that we recognize at least *a* mode of human being that is unthought. Heidegger, and Dreyfus, repudiate presence in favor of absence, because they insist that there can be no "unthought" presence, and they insist on this because they take for granted an over-intellectualized conception of the intellect, just that conception that modern philosophy has taken for granted.

The existential phenomenologists, then, don't go deep enough. In fact, the whole field of the intellect—thought, concept-use, language—is itself a sphere of absorbed coping (to use Dreyfus's phrase). And once we understand this, we can appreciate that it is safe for us to understand absorbed coping against the background of the skills and habits and knowledge that inform our intellectual lives. And we can go farther. We *need* to draw on understanding, thought, and the intellect, if we are to have any hope of doing justice to the phenomenon of presence in all its varieties, including the distinctive presence of that which withdraws or has withdrawn. The baseball player's glove, or the carpenter's hammer, although withdrawn, and in that sense absent, are not absent *tout court*. Theirs is a lively absence, not a dead one. The weather in Outer Mongolia is absent in a dead way to the ball player in Florida, or the cabinet maker in Heidelberg. But the tools that form the body of the athlete's or the craftsperson's engaged living are not absent in that sort of dead way, even if they are withdrawn into the background. They are *there*, after all, for the agent; they are within reach; they are taken for granted, relied on. The baseball glove, and the hammer, like the view out the window, are always available. And this is just to say that they are always present, even when they are in an important sense also absent. But they are present in the way of these things, in the ways of that which is acted with and taken for granted. Theirs is a withdrawing, unattended, absent presence, but it is a presence nonetheless. In granting this, we do not run the risk of over-intellectualizing our lives and activity, our engaged living, for we, unlike the existential phenomenologists, hold back from over-intellectualizing the intellect.

I said that two mistakes blind the existential phenomenologists to the fact that readiness-to-hand is a form of presence, a way things show up. The first of these is the idea that presence (but not absence) is adequately accounted for by the modern account; the second is that the intellect is a realm of detached contemplation.

A basic theme of this book is that presence does not come for free. We achieve presence. We act it out. I hope it will be clear, now, or by the end at least, that this does not mean that ours is the attitude of the stranger in a strange land, and that we must always *strive* to bring the world into focus. The existential phenomenologists are right that that is a distorted picture of ourselves. Living is not a research project. No. As Heidegger would say, the meaningful world is always already there for us. Even to take up the attitude of striving is to take us out of the world, take us away from where we are at home, and set us a different kind of puzzle than we ever face or could genuinely face when we are wrapped up in our daily lives.

But none of this adds up to a reason to think that there is no place for knowledge and understanding in an account of our experience of the world around us; nor does it give us reason to deny that we achieve the world's presence in all its forms. Perhaps an example can help clear up the tension.

Take the phenomenon of reading. When we read, we don't pay attention to letters and words. We don't need to. And moreover, to do so would disrupt the reading. Words, as researchers in this area have learned, are like faces.[7] We no more read by seeing letters, than we experience faces by looking at noses, chins and cheeks. Skilled readers are attuned to word *physiognomy* and this allows them to focus on what interests them, i.e., what they are reading. Of course this is paradoxical. You can't read if you don't see the text, and to see the text you must see (at least most of) the letters. But it is not the text itself—at least usually—that you pay attention to or think about when you read.

There is much that could be said about this example. I want to make three points. First, what makes reading possible is our possession of a very complicated, hard-won set of skills. It is only thanks to the solid embedding of these skills in our lives that textual meanings can be, as they are, immediately present to us. Second, reading always takes place against the background of our more thorough embedding in cultural, conventional, communicational contexts. We have expectations at so many different levels about what will happen in the things we

---

7. See, for example, McCandliss, Cohen, and Dehaene (2003).

read. It is almost as if we are always, when it comes to reading, *in medias res*. To be a reader is to be a participant in a reading pageant that has been going on for thousands of years. It is only against the background of these familiar practices, that reading is even possible. Third, reading does not require that we stand back and contemplate the text—at least it does not typically require this of us—and yet the ability to read rests on the above-mentioned complicated and diverse skills.

As with reading, so with seats, and hammers, and baseball gloves. No, we don't carry the burden of figuring out, all by ourselves, as it were, what is what and how things are to be used. In that sense, we are always already in the middle of things. But this is not to say that our attunement to what there is around us, its presence for us, its availability or readiness-to-hand, is not our achievement. It is only against the background of what we know how to do—a background that we, with the help of others, make—that there is anything there for us at all.

Heidegger and his followers can't come to grips with presence because they don't appreciate that presence is always fragile. They have a fantasy of flow and merging with the world that is, in fact, phenomenologically far-fetched. They grant that absorption and flow can encounter obstacles. We miss a line or misread a word. But from the perspective of their fantasy, this can only be represented as *breakdown*, as the shattering of the spell, as ejection from the zone. But breakdown of this sort is not breakdown at all; it is one of the shapes that our skillful engagement with what we are doing can take. We read, after all, *by* keeping a grip on the letters. It is our ability to keep a grip on the letters and text *without* letting them distract us that is the crux of our achievement. It is our thoughtful understanding and our knowledge that gives us the poise we need to carry on over the rough spots.

Neither the existential phenomenologist's fantasy of absorbed coping, nor the neointellectualist's insistence that our practical skills are somehow best understood as intellectual skills,[8] let alone the outright denial of presence that typifies modern science, have a hope of making sense of the fragility of presence, or of the close interweaving of the practical and the intellectual in our lives.

---

8. I have in mind here Jason Stanley and Timothy Williamson's "Knowing How" (2001) and Stanley's forthcoming book by the same title Stanley, J. (2011) *Knowing How*. Oxford Oxford University Press. I discuss these writers directly in Chapter 7.

I want now to reorient this discussion, and to direct it to work not undertaken in this book. Let us turn our attention to the body in a different way. Consider that organic, somatic field of sensations that forms the ever-present background to our lived achievement of the environment's presence. I mean the tightness in the shoulders or the thrumming in the ears, the aches, tingles, twinges, shivers, vibrations, trembles, chills, tickles, flashes, strains and tautnesses that are, in a way, never absent. I mean that felt constancy of the earth's gravity, the sun's warmth, the night's chill. I mean the felt stretching of the muscles as we rotate the eyes in their orbits.

It is tempting to say of this presence of the body in our lives that it is simply *given*. It comes for free. We don't have to do anything to achieve *it*.

It is true that we don't reach out to the body and so that in that sense we don't even *achieve* access to it. Certainly we don't need to acquire conceptual or sensorimotor skills to bring the felt condition of the body itself into awareness. It is there. It is there independently of what we know and what we judge and what we can do. The body and these conditions of being are an animal inheritance. We are saddled with it. We come to the world with all this.

Perhaps the defining feature of the body's sensual presence is the way it resides (usually) in the background. If we are to hope to bring this pervasive feature of our lives, of ourselves, into focus, then we need actively to withdraw from our habitual engagement with the world around us. We need somehow to let the body itself crowd into the space of our attention and let itself be felt. And this is not easy to do. Perhaps it is one of the aims of practices such as meditation and yoga to enhance the kind of sense of self that arises out of a withdrawal from our worldly engagements.

And so we must recognize that we *do* need to achieve access to the body, after all. Not by reaching out. Not by using concepts. But in a different way. We try to let go of the world to make room for the body.

My emphasis in this book is on the fact that the world shows up. But we are now in a position to notice that to this fact—that the world shows up—there corresponds the fact that *we ourselves show up*. The world shows up thanks to our mastery and exercise of skills of access. We achieve the world by enacting ourselves. Insofar as we achieve access to the world, we also achieve *ourselves*.

Modern political thought begins with the recognition that we don't choose to be born, and we don't choose the conditions of our birth. You don't choose to be born a human being. You don't choose to be born here rather than there, now rather than then, male rather than female, loved rather than unloved, sick rather than healthy, wealthy rather than poor. One day you are here. You are like Gregor Samsa in Kafka's story. You wake up and find that you are present.

This much presence comes for free. And not only that, we can't escape it. We are saddled with it. We are animals. We are organic. We ingest, digest, and excrete, we metabolize, we secrete and we dry out. And we live all of that. We experience it.

I mentioned that modern political thought begins with an acknowledgement of this fact about us. We find ourselves here. And yet—and this is the second fact from which modern political thought takes inspiration—the state has coercive might; it rules over us with force. If there are to be social arrangements that are *just*, if there is to be a form of government that is legitimate, then this must be because we are unwilling to settle for the presence that comes for free, but that we insist on remaking ourselves not as animals, but as persons and as citizens. The challenge, or hope, of modern political thought, is that we ourselves enact a mode of social organization in which we are not merely present, like animals, but in which we are present as citizens.

I won't pursue this digression into the political, but the upshot for us is important. We are animals, and insofar as we are animals, we are saddled with our presence here and now. We are like Gregor Samsa, who awakes to find that he is a beetle on his back. But we are not only animals. I am also a father, and a teacher, and a philosopher, and a writer. These modalities of my being were no more *given* to me than my ability to read and write. I achieve myself. Not on my own, to be sure! And not in a heroic way. Maybe it would be truer to say that my parents and my friends and family and children and colleagues have achieved me for me. The point is that we are cultivated ourselves—learning to talk and read and dance and dress and play guitar and do mathematics and physics and philosophy—and in this cultivation worlds open up that would otherwise be closed off. In this way we achieve for ourselves new ways of being present.

One big difference between these achieved new ways of being and our inherited animal presence is that the former, but not the latter, are open to critical evaluation. You congratulate a person for reaching a ripe old age, or for giving birth, but not for being born. Like it or not, whether or not there are agreed standards of success or failure, insofar as we are persons, we are saddled with *responsibility*. I am not only an animal, I am a father, and so the question arises whether I am a good father.

It is the condition of personhood to be the subject of criticism. Good boy, good student, good worker, good friend, and on and on, like it or not. And insofar as we are persons, our lives unfold in the context of nestings of narrative arcs—we have careers and careers have trajectories. Persons have biographies. Animals have lives. Lives begin and end. Biographies have first acts, and they don't merely end, they have endings.

We are present in the world as persons and we are present as animals. There is the presence we earn, and the presence that comes for free. In characterizing our animal selves I have spoken of the organic and the somatic, but I have avoided the word biological. I want to make room for the possibility that this duality of the person and the animal itself belongs to our nature and so to our biology. The world shows up for us. We cultivate in ourselves the power to bring the world forth. It is our nature to do this. And in so doing we show up not merely as the animals we of course are, but as persons capable of enacting the world through our own skillful exploration and self-cultivation.

1

Conscious Reference

It is not controversial that we perceive only what there is. We do so, however, only when a further condition is met: we only perceive what there is when it is there. Perceptual presence—being there for us to perceive—is not merely a matter of existence or proximity. It is a matter of *availability*. And what fixes the scope of what is available, beyond mere existence or proximity, is understanding. By understanding I mean conceptual knowledge, but also more practical forms of knowledge including what I will call *sensorimotor* knowledge. To see an object, it must be there for us, and to be there for us, we must, in some sense, know it.

Presence as Absence

I begin with vision, and with a somewhat paradoxical claim: Vision is not confined to the visible. We visually experience what is out of view, what is hidden or occluded.

The metaphor that has guided thought about vision is that of depiction, projection, and the *camera obscura*. I reject this metaphor.[1] We do not see the world insofar as it projects to a point.

Examples of hidden presence are ready to hand.

For example, you look at a tomato. You have a sense of its presence as a whole, even though the back of the tomato (for example) is hidden

1. I join Gibson, Merleau-Ponty, and Wittgenstein in rejecting the pictorial metaphor for seeing. See Noë (2004, Chapter 2), and also Chapter 5 of this book, for a more developed discussion of this.

from view. You don't merely *think* that the tomato has a back, or *judge* or *infer* that it is there. You have a sense, a visual sense, of its presence.

In what does the visual sense of the presence of the hidden parts of a thing consist, if it does not consist in the fact that we see them? This is the problem of perceptual presence—or better: the problem of presence *in* absence. The object shows up for visual consciousness precisely as unseen.

Philosophers may find themselves unconvinced that this is a problem. Some will insist that we don't really experience the visual presence of the occluded parts of the things we see. At best, we think we do. I demur: It is bedrock, phenomenologically speaking, that the tomato looks voluminous, that it looks to have a back. Which is not to say that we take ourselves to *see* the hidden parts of things before us. The thing that needs explaining is not that we mistakenly take ourselves to see something that we don't see. The puzzle is that we take ourselves to have a sense of the presence in perception of something that is manifestly out of view.

Other philosophers have a converse sort of worry; they deny that it is true to say, when you see a thing, that you only see the facing part of it. Such a claim, they urge, distorts the character of visual experience. We see tomatoes, after all, not tomato parts! We live among objects, not sense data!

A simple observation suffices to meet this worry. To appreciate the phenomenon of perceptual presence there is no need to insist that we *only* see the face of the tomato. We need only admit that we can't see the tomato's back. How can the tomato's back show up in experience when we manifestly do not see it?

Scientists are not nonplussed by this question and may think they have the answer. *We see what the relevant neurophysiology represents.* We visually experience the presence of a voluminous furrowed ovoid if that is what the nervous system represents. End of story. But that can't be the end of our story. It is definitely a relief to know that neurophysiology gets into the act; it would be upsetting if there were no traces in neurophysiology of important differences in our experience. The trouble is this: neurons speak only one language, that of the receptive field. And there is no way to say "presence in absence" in the receptive-field idiom. Neurons can modulate the strength of their activity to signify the presence of a feature in their receptive field; they signify the absence of a feature by failing in any way to modulate their activity. What they can't do is fire in such a way as to signal that a hidden feature is present.

A somewhat more promising line of empirical research was initiated by Nakayama, He, and Shimojo (1990). They turn away from neuro-physiology and argue that the visual system plays the odds. We see what-ever is judged most likely to have produced the image we receive. If you are presented with a cube in such a way that you can only see one of its faces head-on, you won't have a visual experience of a cube. The odds are just too low, the system reasons, for your relation to a cube to have pro-jected *that* image. When you take up a low-odds angle on a thing, in this way, the system (the visual system that is) lets you down. A striking fea-ture of this account is that it lays importance on such facts as that per-ceivers have a perspective on what they see; that how things look varies as the perspective changes; that how things look carries all sorts of infor-mation about what one is looking at.[2] But what a theory such as this does not explain is how the fact that the visual system represents a cube (or *that there is a cube*) causes you to experience the cube in just the way you do, that is, with just the right presence-in-absence structure. It is this fact—a fact that the theory treats as brute—that needs explaining.[3]

The problem of perceptual presence is very general. Under this heading we can group the so-called perceptual constancies.

Consider the color of an unevenly lit wall. You experience the uni-form color across the surface of the wall despite variations in brightness

---

2. Burge writes: "There is considerable empirical evidence that lower animals have what might be called categorial rather than merely dispositional perceptual representations. Many such representations apply to objective properties like shape, spatial relations, even physical bodies, and are not individually tagged in relation to the animal's needs or point of view" (Burge 2003, 515). What is striking about the work of Nakayama et al. (1990) is that it explains how the visual system can achieve what Burge calls categorial representa-tions by appeal to sensitivity (on the part of the animal's perceptual system, or indeed on the part of the animal itself) to information that is tagged to the animal's point of view (although not to the animal's needs). See Chapter 3 below for more on the supposed con-trast between categorial and noncategorial properties in perceptual experience.

3. I do not mean to suggest that science cannot address the problem of perceptual pres-ence. It is certainly not my view that the involvement of the understanding in percep-tual experience means that perceptual experience is somehow beyond the reach of natural science. Perceptual experience is natural and is a fit subject for scientific investi-gation. Of course. But no empirical theory will get a fix on the phenomenon until it is acknowledged that experience doesn't happen in us in the way that cells fire within us. Experience is active and it depends on the perceiver's knowledge and skillful exercise.

across its surface and despite the fact that variations in brightness make for local differences in color. The *actual* color of the wall, like the back of the tomato, is hidden from view, and yet you experience it. It shows up in your experience.

Or take a look at the window. You see the rectangular shape of the window even though, from where you stand, the window's profile is not rectangular but trapezoidal. There is a sense, then, in which you *can't* see the actual rectangularity of the window; it is present, but out of view. You have a visual sense of its presence even though it is hidden from view.

Finally, consider a different kind of phenomenon: your sense now of the busy detail in the room before you. You have a sense of the presence of lots of people and color and detail. Of course, it is not the case that you actually see everyone in sharp focus and uniform detail from the center out to the periphery. We know that isn't true. It doesn't seem as if it's true. You no more directly see all the detail than you see the underlying color of the wall or the back of the tomato. And yet you have a perceptual sense of its presence.

These features of the world—the tomato's body, the wall's color, the window's shape, the detailed environment—fall within the scope of your perceptual awareness despite the fact that they are, in a straightforward way, out of view, or concealed, or hidden, or absent. They are present in experience—they are *there*—despite the fact that they are absent in the sense of *out of view*. They are present precisely *as* absent.

In what does the sense of the presence of these hidden features consist, in what does their visual presence consist, if not in the fact that we actually see them? This *problem of perceptual presence* is a basic and pressing problem for the general theory of perception.

What stands in the way of our comprehension of the phenomenon of perceptual presence is our reluctance to admit the deep *amodality* of perceptual consciousness. Let me say something more about this surprising and underappreciated amodality. The back of the tomato, the wall's color, the detail in the room, the window's shape—these are all hidden from view. They are present *as* absent; they are *amodally present*. And we suppose, optimistically, that at least the *face* of the tomato, the wall's *apparent* colors, this or that piece of detail, the window's profile— all these at least are given unproblematically. They are simply *present*.

But stop and look again, for example, at the face of the tomato. You can't comprehend the whole of it all at once in your visual consciousness. You focus on the color now, but in doing so, you fail to pay attention to the shape, or to the variations in brightness across the surface. You focus now on this portion of the tomato's surface, but only at the price of ignoring the rest of it. You can no more achieve perceptual consciousness of every aspect of the tomato's front side all at once than you can see the tomato from every side at once. Indeed, no perceptual quality is so simple that it can be consumed by consciousness. (The idea of simple qualia is a myth.) Experience, in the large, and in the small, is complex and manifold; it is always an encounter with hidden complexity. Experience is fractal in this sense. Perceptual experience extends to the hidden. In a way, for perception, everything is hidden. Nothing is given.

Presence as Availability

Here is the solution.[4] The fact that we visually experience what is occluded shows that what is visible is not what projects to a point. I propose, instead, that we think of what is visible as what is *available from a place*. Perceptual presence is availability.

For example, my sense of the presence of the detail in the room before me consists not in the fact that I represent it all in my consciousness in the way a picture might—all the detail spread out at once in sharp focus and high resolution. It does not even seem as if the detail is present in my mind in that way. It seems as if the detail is present in the world, out there, before me and around me. The detail shows up not as "represented in my mind," but as available to me. It shows up as present—and this is crucial—in that I understand, implicitly, practically, that by the merest movement of my eyes and head I can secure access to an element that now is obscured on the periphery of the visual field. It *now* shows up as present, but out of view, insofar as I understand that I am now related to it by familiar patterns of motorsensory dependence. It is my basic understanding of the way my movements produce sensory

---

4. This is the main idea of this book. See also O'Regan and Noë (2001) and Noë 2004.

change given my situation that makes it the case, now, even before I've moved a jot, that elements outside of focus and attention can be perceptually present.

Likewise, my sense of the visual presence of the tomato's back—in contrast, say, with that of the tomato's *insides*—consists in practical understanding that simple movements of my head and body in relation to the tomato would bring the back into view. It is visually present to me now; but because I understand that I now have a distinctively *visual* style of access to it. And the basis of this access is my mastery of the ways in which my movements produce sensory change.

The proposal, then, is this: perceptual consciousness is a special *style* of access to the world. But *access* is not something bare, brute or found. The ground of access is our possession of knowledge, understanding, and skills. Without understanding, there is no access and so no perception. My emphasis here is on a special kind of understanding that distinctively underwrites our *perceptual* access to objects and properties, namely, sensorimotor understanding. We can see what there is when it is there, and what makes it the case that it is there is the fact that we comprehend its sensorimotor significance. Sensorimotor understanding brings the world into focus for perceptual consciousness.

A surprising and fascinating consequence of the idea that we need understanding to perceive is that it is impossible to perceive real novelty. Schubert hinted at this when he explained why it is not difficult to write great songs. You simply need to come up with new melodies that sound as if they are familiar.[5] In a way this is a comment about styles; if a work doesn't make sense against a background of styles, then at best it can only be "ahead of its time." But the point is deeper and more general. To perceive something, you must understand it, and to understand it you must, in a way, already know it, you must have already made its acquaintance.

There are no novel experiences. The conditions of novelty are, in effect, the conditions of invisibility. To experience something, you must comprehend it by the familiarizing work of the understanding. You must master it. Domesticate it. Know it.

I said before that nothing is given. We might say: if anything is given, everything is. If the front of the tomato is given, then so is the

---

5. I thank Alexander Nagel for telling me this anecdote.

back. And the nature of our access to the front is of a kind with that of our access to the back. The thing (front and back) is there for us, present, in reach. Crucially, to be conscious of something is not to depict it, or to represent it. To perceive something is not to consume it, just as it isn't a matter of constructing, within our brains or minds, a model or picture or representation of the world without. There is no need. The world is right there and it suffices. At most we can meet the world. Stand with it, up against it. The tomato is right there, front and back, for us to explore.

Once we give up the idea that *real seeing* is having an object or a detailed scene in all its aspects in focal attention, all at once, we can appreciate more fully what is wrong with the philosopher's objection raised at the outset about sense data. The worry was that we live among objects, not sense data, and that it is therefore a mistake to think that, when we are perceptually engaged with things, we are also aware of how things look from a particular vantage point. In this spirit, Sean Kelly, for example, balks at the claim that you are aware of the trapezoidal perspectival shape when you see the rectangular window from here.[6]

He allows that you can learn to make yourself see the perspectival shapes of things, but he insists that doing so requires detachment and taking up "the painterly attitude." And anyway, the fact that we can make the effort to direct our attention to the perspectival shape gives us no reason to think that we are aware of the perspectival shape (how the object looks with respect to shape) *whenever* we see its shape. It is no easier to see the shape and the perspectival shape, at once, than it is to see the duck in the famous Jastrow figure and the rabbit at the same time. To do that is to commit a nearly impossible feat of divided attention!

Kelly is right that the duck and the rabbit exclude each other; how best to understand that phenomenon is worth careful consideration. It is beside the point here, however. Seeing the window's shape, and how it looks with respect to shape from here, is not like seeing the duck and the rabbit at once; it is like seeing the duck and the lines on paper at once. And it is easy to do this. But what makes it easy is not that it is a simpler attentional task. What makes it easy is that it isn't an attentional task at

---

6. See, for example, Kelly's (2008) contribution to the *Philosophy and Phenomenological Research* symposium on *Action in Perception*.

all. Seeing the duck, and the lines on paper, is not a matter of dividing attention between them; it's simply a matter of having skillful access to them both at once. The world shows up for perceptual consciousness insofar as it is available in the distinctively perceptual way, i.e. thanks to the perceiver's knowingly and skillfully standing in the right sort of sensorimotor relation to things. Awareness extends to that to which we have access and does not require divided attention. We see the duck, and the lines, the window's shape, and its apparent shape, just as we see the object *and* its size, color, shape, etc.

In fact, things are a bit more complicated. It is not enough for perceptual presence that movements of the body can bring now hidden elements into view. After all, movements of the body will bring the hallway outside this room into view, but we would not want to say, without further ado, that the hallway is visually present. Perceptual presence requires a more complicated two-way relation to the perceptual object. Perceptual consciousness is *transactional*, as Putnam (1999) has put it, following Dewey.

It must not only be the case that the perceiver's movements produce changes in the character of the standing motorsensory relation; it must also be the case that changes in the object itself would manifestly perturb the character of the standing relation that the perceiver has to the object.

To put things more generally: An object or quality is *perceptually* present (i.e. it is an object of perceptual consciousness) when the perceiver understands—in a practical, bodily way—that there obtains a physical, motorsensory relation between the perceiver and the object or quality satisfying two conditions:

(1) Movement-dependence: Movements of the body manifestly control the character of the relation to the object or quality.
(2) Object-dependence: Movements or other changes in the object manifestly control the character of the relation to the object or quality.

In short, an object or quality is present in perceptual experience when it is perceptually available. An object is perceptually available when our motorsensory relation to the objects satisfies movement- and object-dependence. Intuitively, we are perceptually in touch with an object when our relation to the object is highly sensitive to how things are with the object and to the way what we do changes our relation to the object.

I refer here to this account of perceptual consciousness as actionism.[7]

This name serves to highlight the importance of sensorimotor understanding for perceptual consciousness.

One upshot of the actionism I am presenting here is that it enables us to appreciate the insights, but also the limitations, of the traditional causal theory of perception.

"The thought of my perception as a *perception* of a continuously and independently existing thing implicitly contains the thought that if the thing had not been there, I should not even have seemed to perceive it" (Strawson 1979, p. 51). This is how Peter Strawson states the basic idea of the causal theory. If I see that things are thus and so, then my visual experience depends, in a fine-grained, counterfactual supporting way, on things being thus and so. I am seeing how things are if things would have looked otherwise had they been significantly different. The challenge faced by the causal theory has been that of placing constraints on the forms this dependence of experience on how things are can take so as to rule out deviant forms of so-called veridical hallucination while admitting the possibility of seeing by means of unnatural prostheses. Philosophers have despaired of providing an analysis of the perception relation.

Until now, that is. Perceptual experience has two dimensions: it registers not only how things are, but also the perceiver's relation to how things are. If we perceive, then, how things look must depend (in a suitably fine-grained, counterfactual supporting way) not only on how things are, but on one's relation to how things are. For this reason, when one is perceptually conscious of a state of affairs, changes in how things look must track both how things are and what one does. As I have argued elsewhere, the hard cases of veridical hallucination that have been the cause of so much concern to H. P. Grice (1961), Strawson (1979), David Lewis (1980), and others, are one and all cases where there has been a marked failure of appropriate dependence of perspectival aspects of perceptual experience on the perceiver's actual and possible

---

7. In other work I have spoken of the enactive or sensorimotor approach; in work with Hurley we speak of the dynamic sensorimotor approach (e.g. Hurley and Noë 2003).

movements. I know of no counterexamples to this reformulation of the causal theory.

To sum up: I propose that perceptual consciousness requires the joint operation of sensitivity to the object and also what I am calling *sensorimotor understanding.* I think of sensorimotor understanding as a species of understanding in general, and so I think of the ways perception depends on the operation of sensorimotor understanding as exemplifying the more general phenomenon, invoked at the outset, that understanding discloses the world to us. If you balk at using the term "understanding" to refer to a form of practical knowledge that is independent of language-use and that is shared by humans and nonhumans, then call it something else. Perhaps we could follow Hilary Putnam's example and call it *proto*-understanding (Putnam 1995, Chapter 2).

Call it what you will, sensorimotor skill plays *(inter alia)* the same function that conceptual understanding can play in mature humans: that of bringing the world into focus and enabling us to lock on to it (in both perception and thought).

Intentionality as a Relation

Perceptual consciousness is a species of intentional directedness. States or acts of consciousness are intentional insofar as they pertain to or are directed toward objects. There is a tension in traditional thought about intentional directedness. On the one hand, intentional directedness purports to be a relation to the intentional object. When I think of my friend Dominic in Berlin, my thoughts pertain to him and not, say, to an idea of him, or an image of him. And likewise, when I see a tomato, or a crowded room, it is the tomato, or the room, of which I am visually aware. On the other hand, intentional directedness purports to allow for the nonactuality of the intentional object. The tension is very well known: if one can be intentionally directed to a nonactual entity, then, it seems, intentional directedness cannot be a full-fledged relation between a thinker/perceiver and a thing.

In the case of perception, at least, I am inclined to agree with those who hold that we should resolve the tension in favor of relationality (e.g. so-called *disjunctivists,* such as John Campbell, Michael Martin and John McDowell).

That is, perceptual consciousness is a genuine form of intentional directedness even though it is a relation that could not obtain without the intentional object.

Actionism aims to do justice to the relational conception of experience (as John Campbell has named it). Perceptual consciousness is access or availability. Crucially, existence is a condition of availability or access. We don't have access to what is nonexistent. However, mere existence is not alone sufficient for perceptual consciousness. For consciousness one needs skills *of* access or, as I think of them, understanding.

Both the object itself, then, and the understanding or skills of access, play an essential role in perception. When there is no object, there is, at best, something misleadingly like perceptual consciousness going on. Where there is an object, but no understanding, there is nothing that even rises to the level of being misleadingly like perceptual consciousness; there is only, in effect, blindness.

Extended Perception

Actionism has a more far-reaching upshot: it allows us to understand what we can call the continuity of thought and experience. Perception and thought are both ways of achieving access to things. Where they differ is in the methods or skills of access that they each deploy. We can get at this issue by considering a problem that actionism might seem to face.

Actionism would seem to have the embarrassing consequence that we are perceptually conscious of everything. After all, your relation to any existing spatio-temporally located thing is such that were you to make appropriate movements, you would bring it into view and were it to make appropriate movements, it would perturb your standing dynamic relation to it.

This unwanted consequence is easily avoided, however. Notice that movement- and object-dependence are conditions whose satisfaction can be measured. My relation to the tomato in front of me is *highly* movement-dependent—even the slightest flicker or blink of my eye affects my sensory relation to the tomato. My relation to the back of the tomato is slightly lower on the movement-dependence scale, i.e. I need to move *more* to change my relation to the back of the tomato. My relation to distant objects is only minimally movement-dependent. Object-dependence too admits of measurement. The slightest movements of the tomato on the table in front of me will modulate my relation to the tomato. Only quite enormous changes in the hallway outside this room will make a visual difference to me; and only an unthinkably large event near the Eiffel Tower would be able to capture my visual attention.

From the actionist standpoint there is no sharp line to be drawn between that which is and that which is not perceptually present. The front of the tomato is maximally present; the back a little less so; the hallway even less so. And to these gradations in degree of perceptual presence there correspond gradations in the degree to which the motor-sensory relation we bear to the object, quality, or situation, is movement- and object-dependent. In general, an object shows up for distinctively perceptual consciousness when the basis of our access to the object is a relation that scores high on scales of both movement- and object-dependence.

From the standpoint of actionism, we are perceptually conscious-ness, at least to some degree, of much more than has traditionally been supposed. This is a feature of the theory, not a bug; it flows from the theory's basic positive claim that presence is availability. Perceptual presence is *one kind* of availability; it is *one kind* of presence to mind. An object is perceptually present when our access to it depends on the ex-ercise of *sensorimotor* skills. Of course, objects can show up for con-sciousness without being perceived. For example, when I think of Aristotle, Aristotle is present to my mind. But he is not perceptually present. He is *thought* present. That is, he is present thanks to a different battery of skills of access, e.g. descriptive, conceptual, linguistic skills.

Importantly, there are intermediate cases. Consider, for example, the case of my conscious thoughts of my friend Dominic in Berlin. I don't mean the thought *that* Dominic is in Berlin. I mean something else. When I think of Dominic this way, he shows up for me in my thinking; he has a certain presence; he is present to mind. Not that he *is* present. He's in Berlin. And not that it seems to me as if he is some-how here. He is present to my thoughts, now, but not as *here;* my sense of his presence, such as it is, is a sense of his presence as far away, *there*, in Berlin. Sartre (1940/2004) calls this kind of intentional act of con-scious thought about someone imaging consciousness.

When I think about Dominic in this way, he is present in my con-scious thoughts, but he is present as absent. It is just this presence in absence that I have argued is a hallmark of *perceptual* consciousness. Phenomenologically, it certainly seems reasonable to say that an absent friend can show up in one's thoughts in very much the same way that the occluded portions of things we see can show up in perceptual consciousness. Dominic's presence-in-absence is different from that of the objects around me; but the difference is one of degree, not of kind. Or so I suggest. And of course the actionism I have presented has the resources to explain this: Dominic scores very low on the movement- and object-dependence scales; but the score is not zero.

What I am proposing is that thought is sometimes a kind of extended perception. Thought can be extended perception when one deploys sensorimotor skills (presumably in conjunction with other sorts of skills and knowledge) to achieve access to something or someone very remote. For example, Dominic shows up for me precisely as standing in a quasi-perceptual relation to me, namely, the relation of being *too far away to be seen.*

If this analysis is right, then the actual intentional object of my conscious thinking, no less than the cognitive and sensorimotor skills that enable access to it, is an essential constituent of my intentional act. In the way that I am now thinking of Dominic, it would not be possible to think of something nonactual. Conscious reference to Dominic is a Dominic-involving act of consciousness rather like a perceptual act. If this is right, then it is not a representational state. In particular, it is not a state in which I represent Dominic *as in Berlin.* Dominic's being in Berlin is a condition of my cognitive/sensorimotor access to him, not something I predicate of him.

What takes shape, then, is the idea that *conscious reference* is, in general, an achievement of the understanding. To see something—that is, for something to show up for one in conscious visual experience—or to refer in thought to something—that is, for it to show up in one's conscious thoughts—is a matter of skillful access to the thing.

To repeat, what I am suggesting is that conscious reference is a relation between a skillful person and a really existing thing. Where there is no really existing thing there can be no access or genuine availability; at most there can be the illusion of such. But the mere existence of the intentional object is not sufficient to guarantee that our thought or experience can involve it; for thought or experience to involve the object, the perceiver must be comprehending. He or she must know how to close the deal, how to reach out and make contact with the intended object.

Suppose that over time I have lost track of Dominic. It's been years since we've been in touch; I don't know whether he is in Berlin; I don't know whether he is alive or dead. Surely I can still direct my thoughts to him, even in circumstances like this!

Yes, of course. But this is a very different way of having someone in mind; it is a different kind of thought, with a different kind of content. It's like the difference between entering a dark room when you know where the light switch is, and entering a dark room where you have no idea where the light switch is. In both cases, we can imagine, you have some good reason to think that there is a light switch. But the fact that you need to search in the one case, but not the other, changes your relation to the room, and the light. And so with my long lost friend. The manner of his presence to mind is fixed by the extent to which I have or fail to have access to him, and also by the kind of skills of access in virtue of which I manage to have access to him.

I do not claim that *all* thought is extended perception. My claim is that all thought is directed to its object thanks to the thinker's skillful access to the object. In some cases, the skills on the basis of which one has access will be *perceptual* skills; in other cases, they will be skills of a different sort (e.g. analytic conceptual skills).

Putnam showed that the ability to be directed to objects in thought outstrips our knowledge of the nature of things. This is a deeply attractive idea. My ability to direct my thoughts to beech trees is not something that I am responsible for all on my own. I don't have the responsibility of being able to single out beech trees by dint of descriptive knowledge of what beeches are. In calling attention, as Putnam did, to the importance of the thinker's situation, i.e. to his or her embedding in an environment (including the social environment), Putnam called attention to the ways it is possible for one's referential powers to outstrip one's personal knowledge. Is Putnam's discovery compatible with the view developed here according to which conscious reference requires understanding? One might have doubts about this: some might read Putnam as demonstrating precisely the dissociation of the ability consciously to refer to beeches and the understanding of what beeches are. That isn't how I think he should be read. Putnam does not give us reason to think that you don't need to know what beeches are to refer in thought to beeches; he gives us reason to think that knowing what beeches are is not just a matter of what is going on in your head. Understanding itself does not supervene on physical or narrow psychological facts about a person. To know what beeches are, in the relevant sense, is to have the right kind of skillful access to them. In addition to the existence of beeches, my access depends on my situation in and relation to the environment—including the social and linguistic environment. My understanding is in part constituted by these environmental conditions. Conscious reference is always an achievement of the understanding, in perception, and in thought. Where there is no understanding, there is only the illusion of conscious reference.

What enables objects and their properties to show up for us in experience is the fact that they exist and that we have access to them. A theory of direct perception requires a theory of access.[8]

This is what I seek to provide: a general theory of access.[9]

---

8. Gibson (1979) appreciated this. He liked to talk of information pick up; picking up affordances of things. This is usually understood in a quasi-information theoretic way. I think Gibson actually might have had something simpler in mind. We pick up affordances. That is, we pick them up the way we might pick up pebbles on the beach. Perceiving, in this view, is not a matter of representing the world in the mind. It's a matter of exploring the world and achieving contact with it. Laying hands on and picking things up. And this is something we can do thanks to our repertoire of skills.

9. Thanks to Alex Byrne and Fiona MacPherson for helpful discussion about the ideas in this chapter.

2

※

Fragile Styles

Presence without Representation

MANY philosophers and thinkers take for granted that presence is representation. We *represent* the world in experience and in thought. Presence is re-presence; we make the world present by re-presenting it; from this standpoint, the main theoretical challenge we face is to understand how we (or how our brains) manage to do this. Representation is the most important entry in the index of most books on the mind in the second half of the twentieth century, whether in philosophy or in cognitive science.

The idea that presence is representation is a bad idea. Here's the conception of ourselves that seems to make the problem we face a problem about representation. Each of us is blind and we are groping; we collect information about what is going on around us; we use the information to build up a *model* or *picture* or *description* of the situation around us. Conscious experience of the world is, really, the experience of what is in the model. Once the model is ready, we plug it in and, voila!, the experience (the illusion) of the world!

There are *so many* problems with this conception. Here are a few:

(1) How you get from a "mental model" to the experience of the world is one of the biggest IOUs scientists have ever tried to pass off on unsuspecting graduate students. How does a picture of the Eiffel Tower in my head explain my sense of the

presence of the Eiffel Tower right there across the street? What is it about the *mental* picture that enables it to do this whereas the postcard in my pocket, for example, cannot? These are not new challenges; they are old challenges that are still unanswered.

(2) Perceptual experience does not seem pictorial. For example, it doesn't seem to me as if the scene before me is present all at once in my visual consciousness in the way it would be present all at once in a picture. This is a theme to which I return in Chapter 5. Some things are in focus. Some are not. Some things are in the background or periphery, other things are central and foregrounded. Granted, the scene does seem visually present to me now, all at once. But this is precisely what we want to explain.

(3) Nature is replete with reflections and images; these just happen. Representations, in contrast, aren't the sort of things that happen. Think drawings, paintings, photographs, descriptions, ceramic models—we *manufacture* these. And in order to do so we must look at, think about, and inspect the world before us and around us. It's hard to see how the supposed existence of "internal representations" in our head or brain is supposed to explain how it is possible for us to experience or think about the world when our ability to do the latter is presupposed by the existence of the former.

(4) We don't need representations. The world is right there. Why inspect a model when you can just inspect the original?[1]

Upshot: We no more represent the world in thought and experience, than we recreate it. We need a new way of thinking about presence.

---

1. The idea that we can let the world itself do the work that any representation might be called on to perform has been articulated by a number of different authors. Kevin O'Regan (1992) argued that the world can serve as an "external memory." Rodney Brooks (1991) has insisted that the world can serve as its own best model. Dreyfus has told me that one can find the idea already in Heidegger. In any case, Dreyfus (1972; 1992), and also Minsky (1985), have articulated the same idea.

The World Shows Up as Available

Presence is availability. This is my main idea. You can't see a solid opaque object from all sides at once. It is a good thing that you don't need to do so in order visually to experience a solid opaque object. We visually experience much more than projects to the eyes. Seeing— conscious experience in general—is not like eating. It is like holding. I can hold you without holding or touching every part of you, and I can enjoy a sense of your presence as a whole even though I only hold your hand. Instead of thinking of what is present to mind as what directly projects to the nervous system and produces activity in the brain, we should think of what is present as what is available, not to our eyes, or brain, but to us.

The front of a tomato; the back of it; the space behind my head; the room next door; the Eiffel Tower; my mother—these are all present insofar as they are all available to me. Depending on where they are located in space and time, the nature of my access to them varies. To differences in varieties of access there correspond differences in varieties of presence.

We only have access to what there is. But not everything is accessible. What constrains access, and so presence, is what we can do— know-how and skill. The meaning of the writing on the wall is available to me if I can read the language in which it is written; the back of the apple is present to me visually from here if I can probe it (say, by walking around to the other side of the apple).

Consider, for a creature with hands there are ways of having access to things—ways of picking them up—that are not available to a different kind of creature. And so with money and language. Money and language expand and enhance the repertoire of what we can do. And so they widen and transform the range of what is available to us. Skills, know-how, knowledge, and understanding—these are the ground of our access to what there is; these mark out the extent of consciousness.

The generic modality of the world's presence to mind is that of its availability. The world shows up *as available,* as within reach. This is why, if we think of what is visible in terms of what projects to the eyes, we visually experience so much more than is visible. (And also so much less!) And this is why it is a mistake to think that we need to represent the world, or internalize it, in order to experience it. As if experiencing were like eating, or as if the only way to hold you were to hold every square inch of you. Or as if the only part of you that I really hold is your hand. I never hold every square inch of your hand either. The world always outstrips what we now touch, or hold, or can take in at a glance. "Real presence," if we think of this as the presence that would be afforded by the existence of detailed internalizations of everything, is a myth. Presence as access is as real as presence gets, and that's real enough.

To repeat, the generic modality of the world's presence to mind is that of its availability. Part of the fruitfulness of this idea is that it allows us to appreciate that what explains *the variations* in the way the world shows up for us—the varieties of presence; its various species—are the differences in the ways we go about achieving access to what there is. I mentioned above that when I see, the world I visually experience does not show up for me as represented in a picture. I said that it is present not as represented, not as internalized, not as pictorial, but rather as *accessible*. Now I add: the world shows up in *visual* experience as accessible, but not as *merely* accessible. It shows up as accessible in a special kind of way, in the way we call *visual*. To the felt difference between visual presence and, say, tactile presence (for example), there corresponds a different repertoire of skills for exploring and so achieving access to what there is.

Too Far Away to Be Seen

It will help to turn once again to my friend Dominic (whom we first met in the last chapter). He lives far away, in a remote city. He is one of my oldest friends. Dominic is present to me now, dear old friend that he is. He is out of sight, but he is hardly out of mind. He is present to me, to my thought, to my imagination. Dominic is in my landscape. He shows up for me. I can't perceive him from here, so his day-to-day changes don't show up for me. But if he were to move to a different city or if, God forbid, he were to come to some harm, this would change my world. For it would change my relation with and so, potentially at least, my access to Dominic.

Dominic is present for me insofar as I have access to him. And crucially, I *do* have access to him. I can jump on a plane, or pick up the phone, or write him a letter, and in these and many other ways, make contact with him. His presence to me now, such as it is, is grounded on facts such as these: that I have the skills and knowledge to make contact with him. Just as money gives me access to the food on the menu, so a whole battery of skills affords me access to Dominic, and it is this in which his felt presence to me now, even though he is thousands of miles away, consists.

We can sharpen these ideas. Presence is a matter of degree. Things are more or less present. For presence is grounded in availability and access. Dominic's presence is *greater* when he is right there before me. It is *less* when he is in Berlin. We can think of our skills, of our know-how, as defining an *access space*. Things can be nearer or farther away in access space. To distance in access space there corresponds the intensity or degree of presence.

We can also speak of the *modality* or *quality* of presence, as opposed merely to its intensity or degree. And this is fixed not by position in access space, but by *which* space of access is in question. Spaces have different structures; their structures are determined by the repertoires of skill that structure them. And to these different structures there correspond distinct qualities.

Dominic is in my thoughts and imaginings. It would be odd to say that he is present for me *perceptually*. After all, I don't see, hear, touch or smell him. He is too far away for that. But it would also be false to insist that my sense of his presence is *entirely* nonperceptual. Being out of view, or hidden, is not in itself an impediment to perceptual presence, at least in some of its varieties. I have a sense of the perceptual presence of the back of the tomato, even though I can't actually see it. I am inclined to say that my sense of Dominic's presence is like this. Using the access-space idea, we can say that Dominic is located at a point in my visual access space that is very remote, and so, correspondingly, his *visual* presence for me is very faint. But critically, my sense of his presence is not entirely devoid of perceptual quality. He is simply much farther away in *visual-access* space than either the back of the tomato, or the tomato's front.

The General Theory of Access

From the standpoint of what we can think of as the general theory of access, thought and perception differ merely as modalities of access. The space of thought, like the space of perceptual consciousness, is an access space. And what grounds the differences here are differences in the relevant skills of access. From the standpoint of the general theory of access, what we call a concept is itself simply a technique or tool or skill of access. As the etymology of the word *concept* would suggest—as well as that of its German cognate *Begriff*—a concept is a technique for grasping something. It is a tool or technique of access.

From this standpoint, thought, no less than perception, is a kind of skillful probing of what there is. And the line between perception and thought is not one that can be drawn sharply. Dominic's presence to my mind in thought is different not in kind but only in degree from the sort of presence he might possess in my perceptual experience. Indeed, from this standpoint one can say that perception is a kind of thought and thought, at least sometimes, is a kind of extended perception.

What seems to stand in the way of a wider appreciation of the continuity of perception and thought is the distorting influence of the representation-idea in the theory of mind. We suppose that concepts are ways we represent the world as being; we suppose that concepts function as elements or constituents of our representations. But what needs to be appreciated—I argue for this in the last two essays in this volume—is that there is a nonrepresentational way of thinking about concepts. Concepts, in this nonrepresentational view, are not so much categories or sets, or prototypes, as different philosophers have held.[2] Nor indeed are they *senses,* as in Frege's view. They are rather skills for taking hold of what there is. To say that perceptual experience is *conceptual,* from this standpoint, is to say that perceptual experience is a *skillful* grappling with what there is. It is not the case that to see an F is to see a bare *x* and then judge it to fall under the concept *F.* Such an idea radically over-intellectualizes our experience. But the critics who make this charge tend themselves to be guilty of an even more intractable mistake, that of *over-intellectualizing the intellect itself.* (See Chapter 6 for more

---

2. See Margolis and Laurence (2008) for a useful overview of contemporary theories of the nature of concepts.

on this.) For these critics countenance the possibility of no other way for concepts to get involved in our experience than in the shape of explicit deliberative judgment. It is precisely the possibility of such a further nonjudgmental way of thinking about concepts that I offer here. Just as I can "get" a joke if I know the language in which it is told, so doves and TVs and armadillos and shades of red can *show up for me*, if I have the skills (the relevant concepts, *inter alia*) needed to bring them into focus.

Don't think of a concept as a label you can slap on a thing; think of it as a pair of calipers with which you can pick the thing up. Seeing something is picking it up using one sort of caliper. Thinking about it in its absence requires that we pick it up, or at least try to, in a different way. If there is a difference between seeing something and thinking about it, it is because of differences in our calipers. Insofar as there are overlapping similarities and kinship between thought and experience, this is because we use some of the same tools in both cases.

A Dynamic Two-Way Exchange

Sensory perception is a dynamic, two-way exchange between the perceiver and what is perceived. When I perceive x, changes in my physical relation to x (whether induced by my movements or by movements on x's part) make a difference to how things show up for me. Dewey, and later Putnam (1999), describe this exchange as a transaction.

Indeed, it is just this sensitivity to perturbations induced by movement (and action) that is the hallmark of distinctively perceptual awareness. Thought, in comparison, is relatively insensitive to perturbations of movement. Dominic's movements (far away) fail to grab my attention in the way that movements of people and things around me would; and my own movements fail sensibly to modify my relation to Dominic in the ways that they would manifestly alter my relation to what is in my immediate environment. This is just to recapitulate the fact that Dominic is very remote in perceptual access space; he's too far away to be seen.

Nevertheless, we can think of thoughtful presence, like perceptual presence, as a kind of two-way transaction with the objects of our thought. This is the central insights of Putnam's (1975), and Kripke's (1972/1980), idea that there are causal constraints on what you can think and talk about. For water, or Gödel, to be present for you in your thinking, water and Gödel, respectively, must have a causal influence on you. Just what sort of influence they have will vary, of course, depending on where you are in the world and your own history and relation to water, Gödel, and the world around you. I happen to know people who knew Gödel, and I know even more people who knew people who knew Gödel. I know people who understand his work, and I know where to turn better to understand it myself. Before me lies a web of people, practices, information repositories, and such like, and all of them are linked, more or less directly, to Gödel himself. It is the existence of such a web, and our ability to find our way along it, that enables us to talk and think about Gödel, and that also, crucially, fixes the quality and quantity of his presence in our thought and experience.

Reflected light is the physical ground of sight, one of its enabling conditions. But I don't *see* light. I see what is illuminated. And so the existence of sociolinguistic practices enable and ground the ability to think about Gödel, Brian Jones, Snoopy, Aristotle, or my great-grandmother. Just as the mediating role of light is, as it were, *transparent,* so the mediation of sociolinguistic practice is also, more or less, transparent. I can think about Frederick Winslow Taylor himself—he himself can be the object of my thought—even though I might need to turn to the encyclopedia to tell you almost anything about him. I use the encyclopedia, but I think about the man. The encyclopedia helps me reach him in thought.

Knowing How to Reach the Object of Your Thought

According to the description theory of reference popular before the work of Putnam and Kripke, a name is an abbreviated description. Gödel means something like: the discoverer of the famous Incompleteness Theorem. In this approach, I use "Gödel" to refer to Gödel because the associated description picks out Gödel; it picks him out uniquely. My reference fails if there is no one of whom the description is true. And if the description truly picks out someone else (because, say, it turns out that Gödel's wife came up with the proof, not Gödel), then that's who I'm talking about when I talk about Gödel.

It was precisely in order to allow for the possibility that I might be referring to Gödel even if most of my beliefs about Gödel turned out to be false, or true of someone else, that Kripke and Putnam suggested that there must be a more direct link between a name and its bearer than that provided by the mere association of a name with a definite description.

Now, according to the access view that I sketch here, you need knowledge to think about things; it takes knowledge for them to show up for you. But I have no truck with descriptivism. Your knowledge grounds and enables your access. It doesn't fix your reference. Access is not a semantic notion. Dominic's being in Berlin, and the fact that I know that he is there, in part explains my access to him and so in turn explains how he can show up as he does in my thinking. But this does not entail that I *represent* Dominic as occupying a specific location or that his presence for me consists in the knowledge of where he is. The fact that I know where he is gives me (or contributes to enabling me to have) access to him. It is because I now stand in a relation of access to him (thanks to such facts as that I know where he is and have cash and a telephone) that he is available to me. Knowledge doesn't fix reference; knowledge enables access.

Varieties of Access

We like to say: you can think about Gödel, about Gödel-*numbers*, about Madonna, and Julius Caesar; you can refer to the Garden of Eden, as well as to the life that might be led by one of your unborn children. What is this strange *reference* or *thinking about* relation such that it is possible both to think about the tomato on the table in front of you and also about a nonexistent greatest prime number?

But the question itself betrays a misunderstanding. In posing it we suppose that there is *one* significant cognitive or semantic relation: reference or aboutness. But there is not. Thinking about things is like catching balls. There are so many ways to catch balls. There is catching pop-ups, catching routine fly balls, there is fielding grounders, and fielding line drives, there is catching balls and strikes behind home plate. And this is to say nothing of catching balls in football, cricket or basketball. These different ways of catching are different activities, requiring the mastery and exercise of decidedly different skills. What counts as success, and also what counts as falling short of success, is very different depending on which of these ball-catching activities you are undertaking. An *exactly* similar point can be made, and must be made, about our thought about thinking. There is no such thing as *thinking about x* such that we can just generalize across all possible values for x. There are many ways of thoughtfully grappling with the world and this is so precisely because there is such a multidimensionality to the kinds of relations (skill-mediated relations) in which we can stand in to things.

Mick Jagger and my father Hans Noë both show up for me in my thought. But each shows up in such different ways! I'm not stipulating this; it's just a fact about my experience. I experience their presence to mind *differently*. We can epitomize this difference by saying that I *know* my father, but I don't *know* Mick Jagger. But this is shorthand for the fact that I have very distinct modalities of access to the rock star, on the one hand, and my dad, on the other. My father is very close to me. I can phone or write him now; I can visit him now if I want to. And I have a wealth of knowledge about him and memories of him. I happen to know quite a lot about Mick Jagger too; I've been in the same room as him at least three times and I know people who know him very well. And to precisely these differences in modalities of access, there corresponds the manifest, experienced difference in their presence for me.

There is variety in the things we need to do to hold on to the objects of our thinking. Old friends, historical figures, mathematical problems, etc.—these occupy positions variously near or far in skill spaces of different shapes and sizes. To think about something is to exercise your knowledge of how to get to it; or, complementarily, your understanding why you can't get to it (anymore, like this, the way you used to, etc.). For a mathematician, to entertain a mathematical proposition is to take up a stance in relation to something you know how to demonstrate (or to understand why you can't yet demonstrate it, or how it hangs together with other results, conjectures, etc.). And to think about Gödel, the man, or Moses, the prophet, is to know how to participate, in any of various different kinds of ways, in the respective practice structures to which they gave rise.

The Fragility of Presence

Another misunderstanding is implicated in, or at least lurks in the vicinity of, the idea that there is a single reference or aboutness relation.

This is the strange and yet somehow compelling idea that meaning is antecedent to linguistic and cognitive practice, that meaning conditions the possibility of such practice. According to what we can call the *semantic* conception of meaning, meaning is transcendent in a sense familiar from mathematical logic. We assign values to primitive names and signs; we fix rules for the assignment of values to well-formed combinations of primitive signs. Only then, having in this way antecedently determined meaning, can we put the language to work (in the service of mathematics or whatever).

But real language is not like this. The question what our words mean is not something that gets settled before we put language to use. It is not antecedent to the application of language to the problems that interest us. Shaping meaning, clarifying what we are talking about, fixing subject matter, this is just one of the things we use language to do. Meanings are not fixed by practice-independent relations between words and things. Nor do we need to step outside of language—as it were to call a "time out"—in order to address questions of reference and meaning that may arise. As if that were possible!

Presence does not come for free; we achieve it. It is hard-won, if it is won at all. Take the perceptual case: perceptual experience is an activity whereby we bring things near us into focus for perceptual consciousness. We peer, and squint, and move, and adjust ourselves, nearly continuously, in order to come near to, achieve access to and stabilize our contact with the world around us. Objects are not transcendent. But they transcend what can be taken in at a glance. The fact of this transcendence bespeaks a certain vulnerability; to know the world, we must move and inquire and explore and exercise our practical and conceptual knowledge. In this sense, we manifest, in our experience itself, our implicit appreciation that perceptual presence is always a work in progress. We turn and squint and peer and take a look again. We hold the curio steady in our hands, we turn it over, and we examine it in detail.

And critically, this is true of thought-presence as well. You think of the person, not the scaffolding that affords you access to the person. But just as the perceiver always understands, implicitly, that his or her relation to the object of sight requires sustenance through shifts of the eyes, head, attention, effort, so the thinker always implicitly understands that his or her access to the object of thought is supported by knowledge, both practical and propositional, and by elaborate practice structures (libraries, history, language, universities, archives, the Internet, etc.) all of which can, in principle, fail. Just as we adjust our perceptual relation to keep the world in view, so we continuously adjust our nonperceptual, thoughtful relation to the world to keep it present for thought.

Meaning is not transcendent. And there is not one reference or aboutness relation. Presence is something we achieve, or, perhaps, fail to achieve. These facts reveal a feature of our cognitive predicament that we easily overlook: presence is fragile and this fragility is manifest; presence is sensibly always at least potentially problematic.

The possibility that there is no Moses—that he might turn out to be merely mythological—is built into the very manner and style of our discourse about him. The practice of talking and thinking about Moses admits within itself the very live possibility that there might not be a Moses. He shows up for us, in our thoughts and stories, as *too far away,* as, in that sense, only dimly present. Do we enjoy genuine transactions with Moses, or don't we? It is not incidental that his existence is a matter of religious faith.

Now compare the case of Gödel, whose proximity in space and time allow for a very dense and vital web of knowledge-based sociolinguistic links between him and us. There is no live possibility for us that there never was a Gödel, which is not to say that it is impossible there never was a Gödel. But to learn of the nonreality of Gödel would cause an upheaval in our Gödel talk and thought practices in a way that the definitive discovery that there never was a Moses would not cause upheaval in our corresponding Moses practices. All the more so for a figure like Hillary Clinton. Only madness or elaborate conspiracies could account for the discovery that there was no Hillary!

In general, fluent mastery of our access skills finds expression in our familiarity with the limits on the exercise of the skill. It is because I can't see the action on the field from here, that I spontaneously adjust the position of my head, I modify my posture, I adjust myself the better to be able to observe and follow and be available for what is going on around me. I exhibit my own sensitivity to the fragility and finitude of my perceptual situation.

You can't see what is too small, or too far away, or too badly lit. We can imagine that there are creatures who see better than us—perhaps they can see more than we do in the dark, or perhaps their power of resolving very small visual differences is better than ours. But we can make no sense of the idea of an infinitely powerful vision. And not because any visual capacity must be grounded in sensory systems which, as physical systems, must be limited in their sensitivity. But for a more abiding and simple reason. Consider: I feel the table before me with my hands. To feel the table is to come into contact with the table, and this means, for my movements to be limited, constrained, and so guided by the table. To learn about something by touch is to come up against its limits and one's own. And so with sight. You can't see an opaque surface and also see through it at the same time; the *in*ability to see *through* the wall is the flip side of one's perceptual access to the wall. We can't really make sense of Superman's vision, because it is unconstrained and, in this sense, unnatural (like a kind of witchcraft). An x-ray vision would be a vision that floats free of what there is around you; for that very reason it can't amount to a way of perceiving what there is.

Seeing What Is Not the Case

My mother looks like a grain of sand when seen from the great height of this building. Question: is this a case of seeing my mother or of failing to see her? (I discuss this sort of issue further in the last section of Chapter 3.) Psychologists like to talk about the breakdown of perceptual constancy. At some point—at some distance, from some viewing angles, in some lighting conditions, etc.—things stop looking to have the properties they have. Human beings start to look like grains of sand. Now, as a matter of fact, my mother does not resemble a grain of sand, not in any respect (size or otherwise). So to the extent that she looks to me from here like a grain of sand, well, to that extent I *fail* to see her. I'm just too far away. But there are considerations that might lead us to the opposite conclusion. I can point to the speck of sand from here and wonder whether it is my mother, or whether my mother can see me from there, or whether she is waving. And it really is my mother, after all, who happens, from this height, to look like a speck in size.

Perceptual access to and contact with what is very far away is partial and insecure. Exactly the same phenomenon is in evidence when we think about thinking, although here what counts as far away, or at the limits of our skills of access, can be very different. Can I think about Fermat's Last Theorem? Well, yes and no. I can name it, and in doing so, I can log in to the sociolinguistic network and secure reference to it. However, I lack anything like a mathematical understanding of the theorem itself; in particular, I couldn't demonstrate it to you; in a very basic sense I don't know how to reach it. I am in the position of a person looking down from a great height not on his familiar mother, but at a stranger. Do I see him? Well, I'd never recognize him were I to encounter him on the ground. At the same time, I can point at him (more or less). So can I think about Fermat's Last Theorem? Well, I can do something like the thoughtful equivalent of pointing at it. For some purposes this counts as successful access. For others it does not.

Presence is access and there is no genuine access to what is not. You can't see nonexistent tomatoes, and you can't think about nonexistent prophets. You cannot experience the presence of what is not, in either thought or experience, because thought and experience are both ways of engaging in a transaction with things. Insofar as there is nothing there—no object of perceptual awareness, no object of thought—then there is nothing to which we have access, and so there is no presence. There is only, and at most, the *false appearance* or the *illusion* of presence. False presence isn't a species of presence, and the apparent visual experience of a nonexistent object isn't a species of perceptual awareness.

The logical possibility of this sort of radical deception allows us to appreciate once again the significance of the idea that presence is achieved and that all human achievements depend on our presence in an environment that supports our weight and enables our action. There is no mark, as it were in the sphere of my subjectivity, that can certify for me that the experience I am now having, or the thoughts I am now entertaining, are *bona fide* episodes in the achievement of access to the mind-independent world! How things are around me either make it the case that the world shows up for me or they make it the case that I am the victim of a grand illusion. This gets decided out of my head.

It is of great importance that the logical possibility of radical deception is *only that*, a logical possibility. Neither the annals of philosophy, nor that of psychology, present even a single case of what Martin (2004) calls "perfect hallucination." The closest we can come, in the real world, to producing perfect hallucinations—i.e. hallucinatory states that are *indiscriminable* from corresponding perceptual states—is in the psychology laboratory. But here what is usually required, of the perceiver, is that he or she *not* exercise the full range of perceptual skills (e.g. you are asked to hold still and fixate a point, etc.). Hallucination in this setting is the breakdown of our perceptual experience; it is not, so to speak, the revving of its engines. So-called virtual reality is another interesting case. Technologists manage, or now begin to come genuinely close to managing, to create alternate situations that we experience as, e.g. an actual cockpit. Yes, indeed. But what is telling here is precisely the fact that the technologists engineer experiences by engineering different realities, that is, different places where there are things for you to look at, spaces for you to move within, and problems for you to solve. Virtual reality no more proves the live possibility of worldless experiences than does the fact that sometimes a plastic piece of fruit looks like the genuine article.

Why is this important? Not because it refutes the anxiety that presence is illusory. And not because it convinces us that this skepticism has no existential bite. That we knew already. It is important because it helps us understand why we are so unmoved by the mere logical possibility of perfect hallucinations. Experiences, and thoughts, are not states. They are episodes of skillful grappling and as such they contain within themselves the necessary possibility if not of outright error or mistake, then at least of slippage, the need for active adjustment or the redoubling of efforts. Worries about whether we achieve access—worries, for example, about whether we misperceive—are not *external* to the experiential state itself, but are, in a way, as with language and meaning, its very modality. Presence is fragile. Always. The fact, then, that we sometimes fail to reach the objects of our thought—that our presences are sometimes merely apparent—in no way shows that we always fall short of achieving contact.

Styles of Mind

According to a bad old idea that governs the way we think about presence, there are two species of the genus presence: there is perceptual-presence and there is thought-presence. The idea has two aspects. The first is that thought and experience are different: there is seeing and there is thinking about (for example) what you see; it is supposed that there is a sharp line here. The second is that these categories—perception and thought—are somehow fundamental and exhaustive.

A good swathe of philosophy gets organized around different ways of thinking about the relation between these two supposedly basic categories. Empiricists argue that perceptual experience comes first; it is that which first makes thought and talk about the world possible. Anti-empiricists (rationalists, idealists, conceptualists) take the opposite view that somehow thought comes first. It is thought or understanding that makes it possible to perceive anything at all.

I have been urging that we embrace a different idea according to which perception is itself a kind of thoughtful exploration of the world and thought is, at least in a wide range of cases (much wider than we might have thought), a kind of extended perception.

My proposal is that the distinction between thought and perception, like the distinction within the category of perception among the different sensory modalities, is a distinction among different *styles* of access to what there is. Thought and perception differ as styles differ. A style is a way of doing something—dressing, writing, singing, painting, dancing. Thought and experience are different styles of exploring and achieving, or trying to achieve, access to the world.

Style has been a low-prestige notion. When it comes to style, we think fashion, pop music or, even worse, orthography. Style is thought to be a domain where people have strong convictions but no good reasons. Style is taken to be a space where we cannot speak of right or wrong, only of how we, or they, say things are supposed to be done.

From the standpoint developed here, style emerges as a fundamental concept in terms of which to make sense of ourselves and other life forms. For what is the mind of a person or animal but, in effect, the sum total, the repertoire, of available ways of achieving the world's presence? And what is the world but that to which the stylish being achieves access? To styles of mind, there correspond types of worlds.

I said above that traditional approaches tend to draw a sharp line between thinking and perceiving. In fact, there is also a way in which the tradition does exactly the opposite. After all, thinking and perceiving, according to one traditional idea, are different ways of *representing* how things are or might be. Such a representation-based theory locates the mind and its explanatory challenges inside the head.

Our style-based approach—according to which perception and thought are styles of activity of achieving or trying to achieve access to what there is—demotes *representation* from its theoretical pride of place. To understand presence, and ourselves, we look not inward, but to the way the skillful person (or animal) performs its life with style.

3

※

Real Presence

WHEN you approach an object, it looms in your visual field. When you move around it, its profile changes. In these and many other ways, how things look depends on what you do. Competent perceivers are not surprised by these changes in appearance as they move.

Of course, objects don't usually appear to grow as we approach them; nor does it look as though they change their shape when we move. Perceptual constancy—size and shape constancy—coexists with perspectival *non*constancy. Two tomatoes, at different distances from us, may visibly differ in their apparent size even as we plainly see their sameness of size; a silver dollar may look elliptical—when we view it from an angle, or when it is tilted in respect of us—even though it also looks, plainly, circular.

Perceptual experience presents us with the world (the constancies) and it presents us with how the world perceptually seems to be (the nonconstancies). A satisfying account of perception must explain how the silver dollar can look both circular and elliptical, how the tomatoes can look to be the same in size and yet different in size. Perceptual experience is two-dimensional, and this needs explaining.

Philosophers have tended to chicken out when it comes to the two-dimensional character of perceptual experience. They deny the legitimacy of one or the other of its dimensions. Sense-datum theorists deny that we visually experience the coin's circularity, or the tomato's sameness of size. At best, perhaps, we infer the presence of those features on the basis of what is present to consciousness. Direct realists, in contrast, may be tempted to deny that there is any sense in which it is *the coin* that looks elliptical, or *the tomatoes* that appear to differ in size.[1]

A solution would be to hold that perception is a way of coming into contact with the way things are, apart from how they perspectivally present themselves, *by* coming into contact with the way they present themselves. I can hold you by holding your hand, and I can see the coin's circularity by seeing what is visible from here (namely the coin's elliptical profile). The question is, how do we do this? In this chapter I address this question, and I try to show that the two-dimensionality of perceptual experience is no obstacle to a direct realism worth defending. But first, I turn (in the next three sections) to a consideration of views that deny the two-dimensionality of perceptual experience.

Denying the Perspectival Experience

Some philosophers reject the perspectival dimension of perceptual experience. Peacocke (1983) has pursued this strategy. He starts from the thought that one experience cannot present the tomatoes as the same in size *and* as different in size, that one experience cannot present the coin as both circular *and* elliptical. He grants, though, that there is a genuine phenomenal basis to the apparently perspectival aspect of perceptual experience. After all, there is some sense in which the tomatoes look different in their size (in their *extensity in the visual field*), even when we see that they are the same in size. He proposes that the elliptical perspectival shape of the coin, and the merely apparent difference in size of the two tomatoes, are not ways the experience presents things as being, but are rather qualitative or sensational properties of the experiences themselves. The experience of the same-sized tomatoes is one in which there are visual field properties that differ in respect of size. Likewise, the experience of the round coin may involve the instantiation of an elliptical visual field property. Such sensational properties of the experience thus contribute to what it is like to have the experience but without being features of the way the experience presents the world as being.

---

1. One philosopher who does accept the duality of perceptual experience in my sense is David Chalmers (2006). He and I agree that perception is in an important sense a "two-step" phenomenon. There are important disagreements between us, though, some of which I touch on in this chapter (not always drawing explicit connections to his work).

What this view captures is the internal connection between actual size and shape and apparent size and shape. Elliptical is the way the profile of a round coin looks when seen from an angle; same-sized tomatoes take up more or less of the visual field depending on their distance from the perceiver. We are not forced to accept Peacocke's account of this internal connection, however. Considerations of coherence would give us reason to doubt that an experience could present an object as circular and elliptical at one and the same time; but there are no similar impediments to an experience's presenting an object as circular but as looking elliptical. Why not say that perceivers are able to see both what size a thing has, and also its apparent size (how it looks with respect to size from here), or to see a thing's shape, and its apparent shape.[2]

There is no contradiction here. Although there is, as we have seen, a looming question. We can ask: in what does the *visual* experience of the coin's circularity consist if not in the fact that it, the coin, actually *looks* circular from here? Can we maintain that we see the coin's circularity when the coin is presented by means of something elliptical?

Another philosopher who denies the perspectival aspect of experience is A. D. Smith (2000). He insists that coins, when seen from most angles, do not look elliptical. This is simply not true, he says. They look round, or perhaps "round and tilted away from you" (172). Smith does not deny—any more than Peacocke did—that there is a definite experiential basis to the claim that the coin presents itself by means of an elliptical perspectival property. He acknowledges, reasonably, that when a student insists that the coin *looks* elliptical to us even though we *know* it is round, she isn't simply mistaken. She is calling attention to a salient aspect of our distinctively visual experience when looking at the coin.

However, Smith does want to deny that this phenomenal aspect corresponds to the way the coin looks. He stakes out a position very much like Peacocke's. What is elliptical is not the way the coin looks, but a sensation, that is to say, a quality of our experience of its appearance. What justifies this claim?

Smith emphasizes that one feels no inclination—not even "the tiniest bit"—to take a coin *to be* elliptical when one sees it (2000, 182). He asserts, "After all, if something really does perceptually look elliptical to

---

2. Michael Tye (2002) has developed a related criticism of "non-representationalist" accounts of perceptual experiences.

me, I shall, if I notice the thing, and if I have no countervailing information to hand, take the thing to *be* elliptical, for I have nothing else to go by." This may be so. However, it leaves open that what explains the fact that normal adult perceivers feel no inclination to take the coin to be elliptical on the basis of its visual appearance is the fact that they do have an abundance of countervailing information. Most of us know that coins are round, and we know that round, flat things change their perspectival shape as our spatial relation to them varies. As a matter of fact, there is considerable evidence that genuinely naïve perceivers— perceivers truly lacking the relevant countervailing information—*would* take round coins presented at an angle to be elliptical. Cheselden (discussed in von Senden 1932/1960) describes the astonishment of a young boy who had undergone cataract surgery at the way a coin changed its shape as it moved; Helmholz describes a similar case of a boy astonished at the changing shape of a locket. More recently, in a similar vein, Valvo (1971) describes a patient who, shortly after undergoing surgery to remove cataracts, perceived as black holes what he later found out to be windows of a house across the street. Large objects far away looked to this postoperative patient like small holes nearby.[3]

Smith gives an additional reason for thinking that coins don't usually look elliptical (or, *mutatus mutandis,* that the tomatoes don't look different in size). The quality of our visual experience that leads theorists such as myself to say (mistakenly, in Smith's view) that the coin looks elliptical is one that, obviously, changes as our spatial relation to the coin itself changes. But normal perceivers do not experience the shapes and sizes of what they see to be changing. This shows that our experience of ellipticalness is not an experience of the coin's *being* elliptical.

I agree that mature perceivers can experience a coin as elliptical without coming to think that it is elliptical. I grant, after all, that there is genuine size and shape constancy. But this does not support Smith's claim that the coin does not look elliptical. The question after all is not whether there is size and shape constancy—I grant that there is—but

---

3. Smith (2000, 35–47) takes pains to distinguish a merely evidentiary from a genuinely perceptual sense of "looks" or "appears." Relying on this, it would seem, one can grant that the coin doesn't look to be elliptical in an evidentiary sense of "looks" while holding to the claim that it looks elliptical in a perceptual sense. Given this, it is unclear to me why Smith thinks that how one is inclined to take things to be is relevant to the question of how one experiences them.

whether there is also *in*constancy with regard to apparent size and apparent shape. As far as I can tell, nothing Smith says rules that out this possibility.

Denying Perceptual Constancy

So much for views that deny or minimize the significance of the fact that we can see the apparent difference in size of the tomatoes at different distances, or that the silver dollar looks elliptical when we see it from an angle. Another strategy for explaining away the apparent duality of experience is that favored by the sense-datum theorists of old (e.g. Ayer 1955): these thinkers do not deny that the coin looks elliptical; rather they deny that it actually looks circular. They don't deny that there is an apparent difference in the size of the tomatoes, but they deny that there is any sense in which the two tomatoes really *look* to be the same size. The basic claim here is that we go beyond what is given to us in perception when we make claims about the shape and size of mind-independent objects.

Now, this line of criticism can be construed in two ways. In a first, epistemological, construal, the claim is that our experience fails to provide sufficient rational justification for the judgments we make about what is there in front of us. This is an important line of consideration, but it is not directly relevant to our discussion. Our focus here is not epistemological, but phenomenological. I take it be phenomenological bedrock that we at least experience the coin's circularity, or the sameness of size of the tomatoes, when we look at it (or them) from a given vantage point. The circularity and sameness of size at least seem to be sensibly present even if we do not take ourselves to *see* them outright. Nor is it the case that we merely *think* or *judge* or *infer* the presence of these features. There is a difference between thinking something is present and experiencing it as present. The way in which the strictly unperceived circularity of the coin is present is decidedly not the way inferred objects are judged to be present. This is demonstrated by the fact that the coin would look no less circular even if one knew, for a fact, that it was elliptical. This is a familiar occurrence when we look at pictures. What is drawn is an ellipse, but we experience it as the outline of a plate, say. We know that, in fact, there is no plate, and so nothing circular, but we still *see the elliptical form as circular.*

Our task, then, is to understand how the tomatoes can be presented in experience as visibly different in respect of size and as looking the same in respect of size. In what does your sense of the coin's circularity consist, when it looks elliptical too? How can the coin look both circular and elliptical? How can we account for the full-blooded duality of perceptual experience?

Merleau-Ponty's Strategy

Let's consider a different strategy for denying the two-dimensionality of experiential experience. Instead of denying one or the other aspects of perception—the perspectival or the perspective-neutral dimensions—this strategy denies that both aspects can be present in consciousness at once.

Sean Kelly (2005; see also Kelly 2008), developing ideas of Merleau-Ponty (1945/1962), grants that we *can* see a circular coin as elliptical and that, in that sense, it can be true to say that it looks elliptical. There is, as he says, a perceptual attitude we can adopt in which the coin really does look elliptical. However, Kelly stresses, this is not our normal attitude. In the normal, engaged attitude, we experience the coin as circular, and it is not the case that the coin looks elliptical when we experience it as circular. The engaged attitude is primary, for Kelly. To see the circular coin as elliptical we must disengage or detach ourselves from the world, or from our engagement with the world. It is quite a feat to be able to do this at all. Indeed, Kelly entertains the possibility that we are able to do this only thanks to the Renaissance invention of the technique of artificial perspective. Whether or not this is true (and I find it impossible to believe that it is), the main point, for Kelly, is that we can't occupy detached and engaged attitudes at once, so we can't experience the coin, at once, as elliptical and circular. In this way Kelly, and Merleau-Ponty, discharge the appearance of duality of perceptual experience.

How, according to Kelly and Merleau-Ponty, do we experience a coin to be circular when our visual access to it is confined to a limited perspective, a perspective from which the visible profile of the coin is in fact elliptical? Merleau-Ponty's account, as interpreted by Kelly, goes like this: when you see a coin from an angle, and you are in the engaged attitude, what it is in virtue of which the coin looks circular to you is that you implicitly register the fact that your vantage point is *nonoptimal*. Your visual sense of the coin's circularity consists in your appreciation that you would need to move, in such and such ways, to get a better view of the coin's shape. In this way, Kelly explains, context plays a *normative* role in perception; we experience the coin *in a context,* and we have a kind of practical understanding that the context guides us in certain ways.

This view faces a problem. We can agree that there may be more or less optimal vantage points on a coin, but this will only be relative to certain purposes. For example, if I want to read the coin's face, or pick it up, or determine its condition, or the year it was minted, then there are more or less optimal vantages points. But vision itself is not relative to certain purposes; seeing is all-purpose. For this reason one cannot maintain that some perspectives on the coin are, as it were, visually privileged. The shape of the coin fixes ways it would look from an infinite number of perspectives, and insofar as we do experience the coin's circularity and flatness, then we experience it as having a shape such that its appearance would vary in an infinite number of ways as we move in respect of it.

Putting this to one side, Kelly's Merleau-Pontyan contextualism would seem to be vulnerable to another criticism: it supposes that we *are* aware, when we are in the engaged attitude, not only of the coin and its qualities, but of the context and the extent to which our relation to what we're looking at is more or less optimal. But if we balk at the idea that we are aware of the coin's perspectival shape when we see it from here, should we not also balk at the thought that we are aware of the ways our movements would improve our view of the coin?

Or we can come at this from the other direction: if one does accept that the engaged attitude makes room for this sensitivity to variations in context, then what principled reason is there to hold back from saying that perceptual engagement with the world makes room not only for attention to how things are, but also to how they look from here? Indeed, I wonder how the proponent of contextualism can avoid saying this. For, we must ask, what is it about my context vis-à-vis the coin that enables me to tell my viewing angle is nonoptimal? Surely it is just the way the coin looks, e.g. that it looks elliptical from here; it is this fact that would guide me to move in order to get a better view of the coin's circularity. What other contextual fact is available to play this "normative" role?

The contextualism we are considering seems to collapse into something like the view I am advocating. In this view, the *way* the coin's circularity is present to me when I view it from a single point of view, is *as available to me* thanks to my implicit understanding that were I to move in these and these ways its apparent shape would change correspondingly. I *encounter* its roundness *in* encountering its elliptical apparent shape together with a practical appreciation that that apparent shape depends on my spatial relation to the coin and would, therefore, be modified by movements. From this standpoint I can readily admit that, most of the time, I'll attend to the coin and not pay attention to how it looks from here. And I can admit that if I were to attend to how it looks from here, then I would need to divert my attention from how it is in itself. But these admissions do not require me to suppose that, in thus shifting attention back and forth, I move between incommensurable *attitudes*. Experience contains within it precisely two aspects, or dimensions, to which we can turn our attention.

This brings us to a third criticism of the Merleau-Pontyan contextualism. Perhaps what underwrites the intuition that the engaged and detached attitudes exclude each other is an idea (entirely correct in itself) about limits of divided attention and also an appreciation of the foreground/background structure of experience. The critical observation, then, is that when I focus my attention on the coin's shape, the elliptical appearance property that would be available to me as the focus of my attention were I to shift to the detached attitude, is present in experience but only as a feature of the background. This seems right, and indeed, it seems right that you can't attend to shape and perspectival shape, or color and apparent color, *at once*. But crucially this doesn't get explained by, nor does it give us reason to give special weight to, a supposed incommensurability of the detached and engaged attitudes. True, you can't attend to the shape and apparent shape of the coin at once, but you can't attend to its shape and size at once either, or its shape and color.[4] You can't pay attention to two things at once.

---

4. This is an important lesson of empirical work on so-called change blindness. The color of an object can change without your noticing it, even if you are intent on focusing on the object. See O'Regan and Noë (2001) for discussion.

Critically, insofar as the world is available to me now in my visual experience, it is available to me both as it is in itself apart from my perspective, and as reflecting my perspective. Perceptual experience retains these two dimensions.

Perceptual Constancy and Amodal Perception

We have been considering examples of what psychologists call *perceptual constancy,* specifically, size and shape constancy. Traditionally, psychologists characterize perceptual constancy this way: we experience objects as unchanged or as constant and stable in their perceptual properties despite the changing character of perceptual sensation or perceptual stimulation. When you approach a tomato, it looms in your visual field—as you get nearer, the size of the image of the tomato on your retina increases; it doubles in size as you halve your distance—yet you do not experience the tomato as changing in size. As you change the angle at which you view the silver dollar, the shape of the image of the coin on your retina changes, yet you do not experience the coin as changing in shape.[5]

We are now in a position to notice that this way of describing the phenomena of perceptual constancy is unacceptable. The question is not: how can our experience continue to present things as unchanged when the character of our experience is continuously changing. Rather, the question is or ought to be: how can our experience present things as unchanged when it manifestly presents them as changing. Perceptual constancy has the character of a paradox: you experience the size as unchanged despite changes in the apparent size; you experience the shape as unchanged despite the fact that the coin looks different in respect of shape!

Let's introduce a new example of perceptual constancy: color constancy. This example will help us better to appreciate the dual character of perceptual experience and so the apparently paradoxical character of perceptual constancy.

When you leave your study, illuminated with fluorescent light, and head out into the day, you don't notice that the book you are carrying, or the skin tone of the person you are talking to, has changed. In a

---

5. This is roughly how Smith characterizes perceptual constancy (2000, 170).

sense, of course, they have. It is this sort of change that underwrites our judgment that, for example, no one looks good by the light of the New York subway, or the color of the pigment you would use to match the book outdoors is different from the color of the pigment you would use to match the book indoors. Of course, we may not notice these changes in color. In part this is because our very grip on color is a grip on something that changes dynamically in determinate ways, as we move, or as lighting changes, or as the colors of surrounding objects change.[6]

Reference to painting here doesn't mean we are taking up the painter's detached attitude. Whenever color judgments matter, it is important for us to pay close attention to the way colors change as lighting changes. If you are buying paint for your house, you'd be advised, for that reason, to bring your paint chips home and look at them in the prevailing lighting conditions at home. To do this would not be to lapse into the detached attitude of the Renaissance. It would be to take up the concerned attitude of a homeowner, an attitude that, presumably, we share with our prehistoric forebears.

We are able to experience a surface as uniform or regular or stable in color even when it is visibly variable and differentiated in its color. Consider a new clean car on a rainy afternoon (as discussed in Broackes 1992). The car reflects lights and surfaces, and yet you can experience it as uniformly colored even as it thus reflects highlights, etc. Or consider a wall that is only partly cast in sunlight. Despite its looking brighter where the sunlight hits it, you needn't experience the color there as different from that of the rest of the wall (even though differences in brightness make for differences in color).

Perceptual constancy phenomena such as these exemplify a broader category of perceptual phenomena, one that philosophers have tended to neglect: amodal perception. Look at an apple on the table in front of you. You have an experience of a voluminous whole. In fact, you can only see the facing surface of the apple. It doesn't seem to you that you actually *see* the whole of it. After all, what could be more salient than the fact that you only see its visible features, its facing side. And yet, in

---

6. See Noë (2004, Chapter 4), for extended discussion of this. I there argue that it is a myth that colors present themselves to us in experience as *simple* and *manifest*. Colors have hidden sides to them, just as shapes do.

seeing what is visible, you have a sense—a visual sense—of the presence of the apple as a whole.

Similar considerations go for a cat, whose body is hidden by an obstacle, but whose head and tail show. You can visually experience the head and tail as belonging to the same cat, even though you can't actually see the part of the cat to which they are joined. Here it doesn't seem to you, erroneously, as if you see something you don't. Rather, it seems to you as if you are aware, in a perceptual modality, of something that is plainly out of view.[7]

We can give substance to the sense that your awareness of these items is not only perceptual, but visual. The distinction between a thought-state and a perceptual one is clear enough. As we have noticed, you don't merely *judge* the apple to be present; it looks to you as if it is. This difference is grounded in the way in which perceptual experiences, but not nonperceptual ones, are highly responsive to movements of the body and changes in the environment. In perception, your relation to the perceived features is *sensorimotor*. What makes the perceptual relation visual, as opposed to some other perceptual modality, is the precise character of the mediating sensorimotor relation. In the visual case, movements of the eye and head play a special role in modulating sensory stimulation. Insofar as you now stand in a relation to the apple and the cat that is mediated by this sort of pattern of dependence of your visual experience of what you do, and insofar as you implicitly understand this to be the case, then to that extent, it seems, your relation to these items is visual. As has been argued elsewhere (O'Regan and Noë 2001; Noë 2002; 2004; 2006), it is the obtaining of this kind of *sensorimotor* relation, and *the perceiver's implicit understanding that these relations obtain*, that is the ground of the claim that, in seeing the visible side of the apple, or the visible parts of the cat, you have a *visual* sense of the presence of the strictly unseen, or strictly *invisible* parts of the cat.

To summarize: in what does your perceptual sense of the presence of unseen items consist? It consists in your practical knowledge of how

---

7. For this reason it is misleading to name this phenomenon *amodal* perception. This term marks the fact that the experience we have of the apple's backside is an experience of what we plainly perceive in *no* modality. Nevertheless, the way in which the apple's backside is present (but unseen) is clearly visual.

to bring those unperceived items into view by movements of the body; in your skill-based sense of their availability.

Now, I propose that perceptual constancy phenomena are themselves examples of amodal perception. The relation of the coin's circularity to what you see, or of the tomatoes' sameness of size to how things look to you, is the same as that of the relation of the apple's voluminousness to what you see. The size of the tomatoes, the actual shape of the coin, the actual color of the wall, these are present in your experience of the tomatoes and the coin and the wall the way the unseen parts of the cat or the voluminousness of the apple are present in your experience. They are present *as absent, but as available to perception through appropriate movement.*

Enacting Direct Perception

Presence in absence is not illusory presence; it is rather a special kind of availability. The world is present, in perception, not by being present (e.g. represented or depicted) in consciousness all at once, as it were, but by being available all at once to the skillful perceiver. And different items are available *in different ways,* depending on the kind of bodily, sensorimotor relation that we hold to them. (For more on this, see Noë 2004; 2006.)

Perception is the encounter with the world from a point of view. The limitations of perspective are therefore constitutive of the perceptual relation. There is no seeing a peach from all sides at once; there is no seeing a wall as it would look in every illumination; there is no seeing the coin's circularity from an angle. The availability of the coin's shape, or the peach's body, or the wall's color, is made possible thanks to our implicit understanding of the way the appearance of these objects would change as we move or would move in relation to them.

The sense-datum theorist was right to this extent: perceptual access to the world is mediated by how things sensibly appear. But this is compatible with direct perception. For what mediates our perceptual relation to the world is only our exploration of the world. The status of the claim that perception is mediated is exemplified by the fact that you can't see the peach from all sides at once. I can hold you, but I can't hold you by holding every single part of you. I can see you, by seeing your surface. You and the world can be available to me thanks to my sensorimotor understanding of the way my contact with you is a kind of contact with the world that is *beyond view.*

Crucially, what mediates the perceiver's relation to the apple, the peach, the wall, the coin, the color, is not a *sensation*—if by this we mean mere qualities in consciousness or *qualia*—but rather skillful contact with the perceptual world. What explains the elliptical appearance of the coin are not facts about my qualia, but rather facts about how the coin looks from here, facts that are determined by the coin's shape and my spatial relation to it, by the coin's place in its environment. What mediates our relation to the world in perception, then, is the world, and what we do or can do. So the two steps can, in a way, collapse into one. Perceiving is *exploring the world.* It is a temporally extended activity. What we call *seeing the apple* just is an episode of exploration. And so we can say that we *enact* the perceptual world by skillful exploration. In this way of thinking about perceptual experience, perceiving is not a way of representing, it is a way of gathering or assembling content.

Sensation in Perception

From this standpoint, we can venture to criticize A. D. Smith's strategy for resisting the Argument from Illusion, laid out in *The Problem of Perception* (2000). The task for direct realism, according to Smith, is to show that perceptual awareness of objects is not mediated by prior awareness of mere sensation (or sensory qualities). Smith argues that the phenomenon of perceptual constancy can enable one to do this. For when "perceptual constancy is in operation, although perceptual sensation is changing, what I am aware of, in the most basic and immediate sense, does not appear to change" (180). When you approach an object, your perceptual sensations vary, but your experience of the size and shape of the object do not vary. It follows, then, that what you take yourself to be aware of, is not the sensations themselves.

This argument rests, as I hope will now be clear, on a mischaracterization of perceptual constancy. I have argued that when you are perceptually aware of an object, you are, *inter alia*, aware of the way it looks. The way it looks, however, *does* vary as you move in relation to it. For this reason, perceptual constancy cannot play the role Smith wants it to play, that, namely, of distinguishing object-directed perceptual states from merely qualitative (sensational) states. It is not that perceptual constancy somehow fails to enable us to differentiate between the object of awareness, with its stable perceptible properties, and the variations in the way the object looks from here or there. The problem, for Smith's account, is that the variations in how the object looks are not a matter of "mere sensation." There does not seem to be a place, in the analysis of perception, for what Smith calls perceptual sensation.

Why does he think that there is? Enter the Argument from Illusion. According to Smith, the Argument from Illusion demonstrates conclusively ("beyond any shadow of a doubt") that the very same perceptual sensations are instantiated in veridical and nonveridical perceptual experiences and they are instantiated in the very same way (Smith 2000, 65). The Argument is as follows: Consider the visual experience of a white wall looking yellow. Insofar as the wall really looks yellow, then, in seeing the wall, you experience yellowness. But this yellowness that you encounter is just the same yellowness that you would have encountered were the wall really yellow. What else could explain the fact that the wall looks to be, precisely, *yellow!* But the yellowness you experience looking at the white wall, is not a property of the wall. The wall is white and the yellowness is a property of your experience.

A philosopher might object that from the fact that you misperceive a white wall as yellow, it does not follow that anything really is yellow. This "sense datum inference," as Smith calls it, is fallacious (Austin 1962; Putnam 1999). Smith insists that such an objection cannot be taken seriously:

> When, in the situation in question, I describe the wall as yellow, I do not just pick a colour term at random. Surely yellowness is appropriate to giving expression to my perceptual state only because that is the colour *I am aware of.* I say "yellow" because I see yellow. When something appears yellow to me, it is, or could be, with me visually just as it is when I veridically see something that really is yellow. The same "sensible quality" is present to consciousness in the two cases. For were it not, why should I make reference to the same colour in the two situations? (2000, 37)

Smith is insistent that we need "to recognize certain experiential facts," to wit:

> When a wall perceptually looks yellow to you, it may be with you ex-
> perientially just as when you veridically see a yellow wall. The experi-
> ences are, or may be, qualitatively identical. The Argument [from
> Illusion] claims that the only way to do justice to this fact is to recog-
> nize that a veridical and a matching illusory experience have a *shared
> sensory character*. When a wall perceptually looks yellow to you, a cer-
> tain sensory quality is realized in your experience whether or not the
> wall is yellow. (2000, 40)

According to Smith, we can be as certain of this as we can be of anything.

Let us agree with Smith that there is such a thing as a white wall's
actually looking yellow. To explain this phenomenon, must we accept
Smith's thesis about sensations? Is it true, as Smith asserts, that the *only
way* to do justice to the possibility of illusion is by supposing that the
same perceptual sensation is realized in an illusory experience and its
corresponding veridical experience?

In fact, we have already considered reasons to be skeptical of this
qualia thesis. Generally speaking, how things look is not a matter of
"mere sensation" or qualia. How things look is a feature of the way they
are. There is no more reason to think that a wall's looking yellow is a
fact about my *perceptual sensations* or qualia than there is to think that a
coin's looking elliptical from here is a fact about my sensations. To say
this is not to deny "the experiential facts." It is to deny that mere qualia
play a role in fixing or constituting those facts. Let us ask: What is it in
virtue of which the round coin looks elliptical? Answer: geometrical
facts about my spatial relation to it, not facts about my internal, nonintentional qualitative states.[8]

An exactly analogous reply is ready to hand in the color case. What
is it in virtue of which the white wall looks yellow? Answer: facts about
the character of the illumination, or about the chromatic properties of
nearby surfaces (e.g. the wall might be reflecting the yellow from the
mustard flowers outside the window). Someone might object that one
would have the experience of yellowness so long as one's brain was in

---

8. My claim is not that geometry is sufficient for experience alone. A blind person
wouldn't experience the coin's shape whatever spatial relation obtains between him or
her and the coin!

a certain state regardless of any environmental conditions. But what does this show? Not that we must appeal to sensations or qualia to explain perceptual experiences, but that we must appeal to brain states.

I want to argue, further, that sensations or qualia, in Smith's sense of *perceptual sensations with no intrinsic intentionality,* can play *no role* in explaining the occurrence of this sort of nonveridical experience. This is so because sensations, thus construed, are neither necessary nor sufficient for the experience of the presence of a perceptual quality. That they are not *necessary* is illustrated by such simple facts as that blinking, which interrupts sensation, does not interrupt perceptual *experience.* A more robust example is provided by amodal perception. You have a sense of the presence of the apple as a whole, even though you only see its facing side, that is, even though only the facing side gives rise in you to *sensation.* That perceptual sensations (i.e. mere sensations with no intrinsic intentionality) are not *sufficient* for the sense of presence of a feature, is illustrated by a consideration of someone who has adapted to reversing goggles. The goggles affect incoming stimulation so that an object on the left stimulates the eye and brain as an object on the right normally would. That is, the object gives rise to a *right*-sensation, even though it is on the left. After adaptation, however, the object looks as though it *is* on the left, even though it continues to produce right-sensations (that is, sensations that would normally be produced by an object on the right). The quality experienced varies even though the sensation does not.

If the occurrence of mere sensation does not explain the experience of location of an object in the visual field, what does? An object on the left is one whose appearance changes in precise ways as one moves in relation to it. What fixes the experience of an object *as on the left* is not the intrinsic character of sensations, but the perceiver's implicit grasp on the way *how the object looks* would vary as he or she moves. Adaptation to reversing goggles, then, is a matter of figuring out the patterns of sensorimotor dependence governing your relation to the object, not a matter of having certain kinds of feelings (O'Regan and Noë 2001; Hurley and Noë 2003; Noë 2004).

And so for other kinds of perceptual experience. In what does your visual sense of the cubicalness of a cube consist? It consists in your implicit expectation that its appearance would change in the characteristically cubical way as you move in relation to it. Sides come in and out of view, vertices come in and out of view in the ways definitive of cubical-ness. Importantly, there is no *cube* sensation, just as there is no sensa-tion as of leftness. To experience something as a cube, or as on the left, is to experience it as exhibiting a characteristic *sensorimotor* profile. Likewise, the hidden parts of the apple and the cat are present, in vi-sion, as accessible, not as *given* (as it were).

What these considerations show is that how things visually seem to be is not explained by appeal to sensations (at least if we understand these nonintentionally as Smith does).[9] We can't explain the qualitative features of experiential states (veridical or nonveridical) by supposing that they depend on the instantiation of sensations in consciousness.

If it is possible to do justice to the possibility of illusion without ap-pealing in the way Smith does to mere sensation, then the mere possi-bility of illusion doesn't imply anything about the role of qualia or perceptual sensation in illusion. The Argument from Illusion, it would seem, leaves us where it starts, with the observation that illusion is pos-sible, i.e. there needn't be anything in the character of one's experience to enable one to tell whether the qualities one seems to see are really present or not.

Enactive Realism

A main idea of a central variant of what is known as disjunctivism in the philosophy of perception is that perceiving is a direct relation with situations and things. For this reason, the perception of the wall's yel-lowness and the corresponding hallucination could not involve the oc-currence of one and the same conscious state. We experience the wall's yellowness only when the experience is veridical. The burden on dis-junctivism is that of making intelligible that the two episodes are differ-ent, even though, as far as the subject is concerned, they present or seem to present the world as being the same way. How can percep-tual experience depend, in this way, on something external to the perceiver?

---

9. If we allow for a conception of sensations as themselves intentional, that is, as world-directed, then it is unclear what explanatory work they could be called on to do. For sensation thus conceived would in effect be perceptual experience, but that is precisely that for which we seek an explanation.

I suspect that what makes it difficult to see how the disjunctivist could be right is the fact that we, and perhaps the disjunctivist him or herself, tend to think of experiences as inner representations.[10]

If perceptual content is representational content—that is, if it presents to consciousness ways the world might be—then it is hard to see how the perception/hallucination pair can fail to share a common content. A perception and its corresponding perfect hallucination disagree, after all, not in how things are presented as being, but in whether things are that way.

We have been considering reasons to give up the idea that experiences are representational in this way. In the view of experience developed here, perceivings are not *about* the world; they are episodes of contact with the world. This standpoint makes it easier to find the disjunctivist alternative intelligible. If perceivings are understood on the model of touchings, then we can think of the content of the experience as given precisely by what we touch. A hallucinatory experience may be indistinguishable from the veridical experience, but not because they share the same content, but because it is *as if they do*. A critic may be entitled to demand of the disjunctivist that he or she explain how this *apparent content* is possible. I have tried to do this. But what the critic is not entitled to do is insist that the *only way* to explain the indistinguishability of the two experiences is by insisting that they share the same content (or, to put the same point in a different way, that they are of the very same kind). The account presented here seeks to explain the indistinguishability of experiences of seeing and hallucinating without any assumption of shared content (that is, without any assumption of shared contact with the world).[11]

The disjunctivist thinks (indeed, *must* think) of perceptual experience according to what John Campbell (2002) calls "the relational concep-

---

10. I find that there is at least a tension in the work of McDowell on this point. Insofar as McDowell holds that perceptual experiences and corresponding thoughts can share one and the same content, then it would seem that he is committed to the idea that perceptual content is representational.

11. Some resistance to disjunctivism may stem from the worry that the disjunctivist is dogmatic in *disallowing* the demand for an explanation of the hallucinatory appearance of perceptual content. At this late day in history, we tire of being scolded for being in the grip of the Cartesian picture. In fact, the disjunctivist needn't adopt the scolding attitude. What the skeptic (or critic of disjunctivism) is not entitled to is the *assumption* that there is no such thing as *the mere appearance of content* or that any *appearance of content* implies that there is content. These assumptions are tantamount to the assumption of the falsehood of disjunctivism.

tion of experience." According to this conception, perceptual experiences are relations between a perceiver and the environment. Perceptual experience, in this understanding, is not intentional. The sense-datum theorist also thinks of perception as a nonintentional relation to the world, for the sense-datum theorist thinks of perception as a mode of direct awareness of sense data. From the fact that one experiences something as yellow, it follows that yellowness exists in one's consciousness. In the relational conception of experience, perceivings are likewise relations to the world in that what we experience when we have a perceptual experience of the wall's yellowness is just the wall's yellowness.

Campbell criticizes some formulations of disjunctivism (e.g. McDowell's) for taking intentionality for granted. The world reveals itself to us in perception, and, according to Campbell, it is perception—conscious awareness—that first makes thought and talk about the world possible. For this reason, thought—even world-involving thought—cannot provide content for perceptual experience. Perceptual awareness of things in the world is a more primitive kind of world-directedness than we find in representational thinking.

Understood one way, this seems right. Perceiving is a relation between the perceiver and the world. Perception is nonrepresentational in the sense that perceivings, as I have urged, are not *about* the world, they are episodes of contact with the world. And this contact can surely enable us to think about the world with which we thus make contact. Understood in a different, more foundationalist or empiricist way, however, Campbell's insistence of the primitiveness of conscious awareness strikes me as unjustified. The fact that perceiving is a direct relation to the world—something we cannot do in the world's absence—does not in itself give us a reason to think that perception is *prior* to thought. For a relational conception of experience leaves open the possibility that only thinkers are able to establish or maintain the right sort of perceptual contact with the world.

In fact, I think, something like this is precisely the case. According to the *actionist* (or enactive) direct realism that I am developing here, there is no perceptual experience of an object that is not dependent on the exercise, by the perceiver, of a special kind of knowledge. Perceptual awareness of objects, for actionist-direct realism, is an achievement of the sensorimotor understanding.

We can bring out the immediate relevance of this proposal by considering Campbell's claim that perception enables us to confront an individual substance itself (2002, 116). His example: You hear your neighbors through the wall. What you hear enables you to hypothesize the locations of, for example, the dishwasher and the dining table. You form a conception of that which produces such and such sounds at such and such times, that is, you form a conception of the dishwasher as that which plays a certain functional role as the source of sounds, etc. When you finally get to go next door and actually see the dishwasher, you encounter the individual substance itself and so are able to form a conception that is not the conception of an hypothesized object, of something that played a certain functional role. You move from a conception of the object in terms of its dispositions, to a *categorical* conception of the object as the base of those dispositions, a conception of it as the thing that stands before you.

The contrast between a dispositional and a categorical conception of the object is clear; but I question whether this contrast gets marked in perceptual experience as distinct from thought. There can be no doubt that perception enables us to encounter objects as the categorical ground of, say, the way they look or sound. We can be confident that our experience of an apple is not a kind of unconscious inference to that which gives rise to the different appearances of the apple. Experience is not ratiocinative in this way. Nevertheless, as I have been at pains to argue, these facts don't take anything away from the fact that the apple, as an individual substance, is beyond what we can take in at a glance, from a perspective. Insofar as the apple as an individual substance is experienced as present in our experience, it can only be as *present but absent,* that is, as absent, but available. And the nature of the apple's availability is determined by practical knowledge of the sensorimotor relations in which we stand to the apple.

In invoking the role of practical knowledge in this way I am not suggesting that *direct* awareness of the apple as an individual substance is unattainable. To the contrary, the point is that the apple's direct presence to perception can never be more than an awareness of it as appearing this way or that and as available in this or that way. Objects, as categorical grounds of their appearance properties, are given to us *by way* of those appearance properties. There's no avoiding this fact; it is the perceptual predicament.

The heart of my claim is that sensorimotor understanding belongs to the complicated adjustments necessary for attaining and maintaining perceptual contact with the world.[12] The claim is not that the relevant understanding gets exercised in the construction of a representation (a thought, or anything else). Perceiving, in this view, is not representational and so it is not thoughtful in the sense in which thoughts are (or might be supposed to be) representations. Sensorimotor understanding, like computational or neural processing in the brain, enters into perceiving not by giving rise to representations of what is seen in us, but by enabling us to occupy a vantage point from which it is possible to see. Sensorimotor understanding is the background skill thanks to which we succeed in making direct contact with the world, just as it is the baseball player's skill that enables him to make direct contact with the ball.

This is my picture of the way sensorimotor skills enter into perceptual experience. They are, as it were, skillful ways of achieving contact with situations and things. They are not, as it were, elements of the medium of representation. They are not intermediaries. They characterize our manner of openness to the world (to put the point McDowell's way). This conception undergirds my proposed way of resisting the argument from hallucination in the last section. What explains the possibility of perfect hallucination is the fact that it is possible for our sensorimotor skills to get triggered by the wrong thing, or by nothing at all. That is, this is what can explain the fact that we might sometimes be unable to discriminate our current situation from one of genuinely perceiving. The view explains the possibility of perfect hallucination with reference to the mere exercise of the relevant skills and it does so, very importantly, without supposing that the exercise of such skills alone suffice to determine the *nature* of our experience, e.g. whether it is perceptual or merely hallucinatory. There is all the difference in the world between the nature of a hallucination and an episode of seeing.

What is at stake in my disagreement with Campbell, really, is a controversy about the *character* of perceptual phenomenology. Just what are perceivers committed to in a naïve realist conception of their perceptual

---

12. Compare this with what Campbell writes: "It is not that the brain is constructing a conscious inner representation whose intrinsic character is independent of the environment. It is, rather, that there is a kind of complex adjustment that the brain has to undergo, in each context, in order that you can be visually related to the things around you; so that you can see them, in other words" (2002, 119). I am making exactly the same kind of point, but extending it to the role of understanding in perceptual experience.

relation to the world? Campbell emphasizes that we think of ourselves, in perception, as confronted by individual substances themselves, as categorical grounds of experience. It is the fact that perception gives or at least seems to give us the world *this way,* that first enables us to form a conception of objects as independent of us. It is certainly no part of our naïve phenomenology that we take ourselves to represent the perceived scene in consciousness. We take the scene—*what we see*—to be out there in the world and to be, in its basic features, independent of us. This is right, but it is only a partial characterization of our naïve phenomenology. Perceptual phenomenology is more complicated than that. This is the point of my extended discussion, at the outset of this chapter, of the two-dimensionality of perceptual experience as well as the discussion, in earlier chapters, of the manifest fragility of experience. It is no less rock bottom in our phenomenology that we take ourselves, when we make perceptual contact with the world, to do so from a standpoint or viewpoint. When we encounter the world, we do so by encountering how it perceptually appears *from here.* We experience how things are, and we experience how they merely seem to be. It is true that, for example, when we see colors, we take them to be *simple and manifest* in the sense that we naïvely take them to be *intrinsic properties of surfaces of objects.* But *that* doesn't imply that we take ourselves, when encountering them, to enjoy a wholly unmediated contact with them. Likewise, when we experience the shape of something (a tomato, say, which has a rather distinctive ovoid-with-a-furrow shape), we take the shape to be an *intrinsic property of the object,* but we don't take ourselves, in encountering the shape, to be encountering *all of it,* in a way that is not mediated by perspective. When we see the tomato, we experience its shape, but we experience the shape as *partially hidden* as a result of our vantage point.[13]

For this sort of reason, the task for the theory of perception, as I understand it, is to explain the sense in which we are able to encounter the world of mind-independent things out there when we only have ready

---

13. Chalmers (2006) argues that *primitivism* comes closest to giving a phenomenologically adequate account of visual experience of color. This can't be right, I think, not if primitivism requires that we take our perceptual encounters with colors to be, as Chalmers puts it, *edenic.* Even in the Garden of Eden, before tasting of the Tree of Illusion and the Tree of Science, our experiences of color, as our experiences of shape, were encounters with natures that *transcend* the episodes of encounter. Colors, like shapes, always have hidden aspects.

access to limited bits of things. To explain this, I believe, we need to bring in our understanding. To gain the world as it is apart from us in terms of how the world is given to us, we need to *understand* what we see.

At this point, the actionist approach may seem to come perilously close to conceptualism. According to conceptualism, what enables experience to "hook onto" the world is the perceiver's conceptual knowledge. Our experience presents us with deer and yellow walls only because we have concepts of those things and so can appreciate what we see as glimpses of them. Conceptualism, however, faces the charge that it over-intellectualizes the mind, and moreover, that it makes it mysterious how mere animals can have perceptual experience. The actionist approach agrees with the conceptualist that what enables the barrage of sensory stimulation to rise to the level of perception is our possession of a certain kind of knowledge, but the knowledge in question is not straightforwardly conceptual, it is sensorimotor. The charge of over-intellectualizing is thus answered, in two distinct ways. First, sensorimotor knowledge is knowledge of the way sensory stimulation varies as we move; it is knowledge that we share with nonlinguistic creatures. Second, sensorimotor knowledge gets brought to bear in experience not in the form of judgment or belief or representation construction. The knowledge is practical, and we *use* it to gain and maintain contact with the world.

The actionist approach, moreover, explains something the conceptualist can't, namely, the distinctively *sensory* way in which, in experience, the world is present.

I have proposed that we think of sensorimotor knowledge as a kind of basic conceptual (or *proto*-conceptual) knowledge (Noë 2004). The significance of that proposal is not to assimilate perceiving to the exercise of the intellect, to representational thought, but to assimilate thought and conceptuality to nonrepresentational perceiving. In one way of thinking of object-dependent thoughts, these are representational states that one can only attain by standing in a certain kind of relation to the world. But in another way of thinking about them, they are (like perceivings) episodes of *grappling* with the world itself. Thought, in this approach, is not prior to perception; nor is perception prior to thought. Some thinking is perceptual and some perception is thoughtful.

A Puzzle about Veridicality

In this chapter I have proposed that we think of perceptual experiences as temporally extended patterns of engagement with the world, not as things that happen in us. We enact perceptual experience; it doesn't happen to us. Perceptual experiences, then, should not be thought of as representations, as internal states that are *about* a scene. Rather, they are episodes of contact *with* a scene. This nonrepresentationalist conception of experience squares with perceptual phenomenology, I would say. After all, perceptual experiences don't *feel* like representations. It doesn't seem to us, when we see, as if *what we experience* is represented in our head. Rather, it seems to us as if what we see is *out there* in the world. And it seems to us as if we have a special kind of *access* to what is out there. Our sense of the presence of objects and properties around us, in perceptual experience, is understood in terms of our being skillfully poised to *reach out and grasp* them. Instead of thinking of perceiving on the model of seeing, which is in turn understood according to a kind of quasi-photographic or optical-projective model, we should think of perceiving in terms of touching.

Perceptual experiences are not representations, but this fact does not mean that it is inappropriate to speak of their veridicality or nonveridicality. It does mean we need a new model of what this veridicality or nonveridicality can amount to. In a representationalist conception of perception, the question is, in effect, one of matching or satisfaction. How must things be for things to be the way this experience represents them as being? What can we say about the nature of veridicality if we reject the idea that perceptual experiences are representational?

To take steps towards such an account, consider the visual experience of stars in the night sky. When you look up in the night sky, you don't actually visually experience *the stars;* what you see, rather, are points of light in the night sky, points of light you reasonably take to be stars (or to be marks or signs or traces of stars). The stars themselves do not enter into your experience. The direct theory of perception fails for the seeing of stars in the night sky. We can see why this is so by considering that, for one's experience of the night sky to be veridical (as we would like to say), there's no requirement that stars be points of light, or that they really look like points of light, or that they be located where we seem to see them. That's why the fact that stars may have gone

extinct millions of years ago does not put the lie to our current experience of the night sky.

The case of seeing stars is one where perceptual constancy breaks
down. This breakdown introduces nonveridicality. Perceptual constancy also breaks down, for example, when you look down from the
height of a very tall skyscraper at cars and people below. The people
look to be the size of ants! That is to say, you can't really experience *the
people* from the top of the skyscraper. After all, there's nothing in the
least ant-like about people (in respect of size). That they look the size of
ants is intelligible, of course. This means, roughly, that what you see
takes up about the same amount of visual field as an ant would when
looked at from a normal upright position. What can't be denied is that
this is an *incorrect* experience of the people. For what *would* make such
an experience veridical? The actual presence of ant-sized people!

These cases of breakdown in perceptual constancy can be con-
trasted with cases where there is no such breakdown. Consider our example of the silver dollar seen from an angle. You do experience the
coin's circularity (or so I have argued) even though the coin looks elliptical from your viewpoint (or so I have argued). Despite the discrep-
ancy between the coin's shape and the way it looks, there's no element
of nonveridicality in your experience of the coin. Elliptical is just the
way circular coins look when seen from an angle. Likewise, when you
experience a wall as uniformly colored, even though there are visible
variations in brightness across the surface of the wall, as a result of un-
even illumination, you do not *misperceive* the wall's color.

But now the puzzle begins to take shape. What licenses us to say
that there is no misperception in the case of the coin and the wall, but
there is in the case of the stars and the people down below? In both
cases, you might insist, the very same sorts of causal processes join us
to distal events and objects. If *elliptical* is just the way circular coins look
from an angle, and if *variegated in brightness* is just the way a uniformly
colored wall looks when light falls on it in this way, then why can we
not say that *ant-like* is just the way people look from this height, or *point-
of-light-like* is just the way stars look from this distance? How can we
defend against the charge that we are simply prejudiced and so arbitrary in our attitude to large distances (or time scales)?

Traditional thought about perception has been governed by an optical projective conception of seeing that is closely allied to the idea that

experiences are representations. If you take this conception of experience for granted as a starting point, then indeed it is impossible to find a principled way of distinguishing between the sort of perceptual failure we experience when looking down on people from great heights and the normal, veridical variations in perspective that we experience when looking at objects from different angles. I would suggest that this is a reason—a further reason—to give up the optical-projective conception of visual experience. In thinking about how we might do this we can come back to our problem about veridicality with which we began.

Consider: I have insisted that perception can be thought of as two-step insofar as we perceive things by perceiving their appearances from a location. It is sometimes useful to think of appearances in terms provided by projective geometry. For example, it helps to explain why a round thing looks precisely *elliptical* when seen from a certain angle. But from this it does not follow that looks are projections or that we should think of experiences as like internal screens on which the outer world is projected. In this chapter I have proposed that we think of see-ings as like touchings. In this analogy, seeing how things look is a way of coming into contact with them, it is a way of grasping them. This is why the things themselves enter into visual experience. We see—that is to say, we come into contact with—*them*.

Now, we have considered different ways of failing to establish and maintain contact with things in perception. I have argued, for example, that if you don't *understand* what you see—in the sensorimotor sense I have laid out—then sensory stimulation caused by an object won't rise to the level of contact. In the context of the present discussion, we come upon another form of *failure* to make or preserve contact. When we look up at the night sky, I argue, we just don't succeed in making contact with the stars although we do succeed in making contact with the lights in the night sky. The stars are just too far away! Ditto for the people down below on the ground. In contrast, for the skillful perceiver, a glimpse of a coin from an angle suffices to enable him or her to grab hold of the coin visually, as it were. Of course if you move the coin far enough away, it ceases to look circular, or elliptical, and becomes little more than a spot. This reveals not that coins seen from such and such a distance look like spots, but rather, that at such and such a distance, one's ability to see the coin—to maintain contact with it—breaks down.

It is relevant that most cases of nonveridical perception are cases of *merely partial* nonveridicality. You misperceive the spoon as bent in water, for it isn't bent. But in thus misperceiving the spoon, you do succeed in seeing the spoon. In exactly the same way, you may fail to visually experience the stars, but not because you are hallucinating. You *do* experience the lights in the night sky. You *are* in contact with them. For example, when you move your eyes away, they go out of view. You modulate your relation to them in this and many other ways. For the vast majority of cases of nonveridical perception, the world *is* at hand, and is present, thus, as a partner in the experience, as content for the experience.

Perfect hallucination (to use Martin's 2004 phrase again) is altogether different from ordinary misperception. For in perfect hallucination, the mistake is more radical. It is not that you misidentify what you are in contact with; it is that you take yourself to be encountering the world (to be having an experience), when you are not. The mistake, then, is that you take yourself to be *in contact* with something, when you are not. And there is no need, as argued earlier in this chapter, to explain that possibility by supposing that you are, in such a case, *really* in contact with something else. There need be nothing there, and so no real experience.

In an actionist, or enactive, nonrepresentational approach to experience, then, an experience is nonveridical when what you contact is not what you might have thought. Perfect hallucination is only misleadingly described as nonveridical perceptual experience. For in such a case there is no genuine experience of the world at all. There only seems to be.

Perception is a mode of encounter with how things are by encountering how they present themselves to a vantage point. Perceptual experiences are ways of coming into contact with the world, not ways of building up or constructing representations of ways things are or might be. Perception is, in this sense, a nonintentional relation to the world. But it is not a brute, external relation. It is one that our brains, and our minds, enable us, with considerable effort, to achieve.

4

※

Experience of the World in Time

LOOK at a tomato. It is present to you, as a whole, now, even though
parts of it are hidden in space. Notice, in particular, that you now have
a perceptual sense of the presence of the tomato's back even though you
do not now see it. Objects—even tomatoes—are, in a sense, timeless—
they exist, all at once, whole and integrated. Indeed, it is just this fact
about objects—their timelessness—that makes it puzzling how we can
experience them as we do. In the language of traditional philosophy,
objects are transcendent; they outstrip our experience; they have hidden parts, always. When you perceive an object, you never take it in
from all sides at once. And yet you have a sense of the presence of the
object as a whole at a moment in time. In what does this perceptual
sense of the object's presence consist?

Perceptual presence is *the* problem for the theory of perception. We
don't advance toward a solution by observing that we judge, or infer, or
guess that the back of the tomato is present, that we don't really *see* it.
First, that we don't actually see the back of the tomato is our starting
point. The problem is to understand in what our perceptual sense of the
thing's hidden presence could consist if it does not consist in the fact that
we see it. Second, as a phenomenological matter, there is a difference
between *thinking* that something out of view is present (e.g. that there is
money in the purse), and its *looking* as if something out of view is present
(e.g. that the tomato is not a mere tomato-façade). What we want is an
account of the *perceptual* presence of that which is not perceived.

The solution to the problem of perceptual presence is achieved by
noticing that the way the unseen portion of the tomato is visually pres-

ent is not, as it were, as somehow mysteriously *seen without being seen,* or as *represented visually without being seen.* Rather, the back of the tomato is present, now, in that it is available now. *We have access now to it.* And not just any old access. We experience the presence of what is out of view by understanding, implicitly, that our relation to what is out of view is such that movement of the eyes, or the body, brings it into view, and such that movements of the thing itself make a sensory difference to what we experience. The hidden portions of the object are present in experience now, even though we don't now see them, because we are now coupled to them in a special, immediate, familiar, sensorimotor manner. Sensorimotor coupling is an achievement of contact. It is the achievement of contact in which perceptual awareness consists.

Andy Clark (2006) has recently questioned whether this sort of *presence-as-skill-based-access* view can be right. He begins by adducing an example of Sean Kelly's:

> There you are at the opera house. The soprano has just hit her high note—a glass shattering high C that fills the hall—and she holds it. She holds it. She holds it. She holds it. She holds it. She holds the note for such a long time that after a while a funny thing happens: you no longer seem only to hear it, the note as it is currently sounding . . . in addition, you also seem to hear something more . . . the note now sounds like it has been going on for a very long time . . . what you hear no longer seems to be limited to the pitch, timbre, loudness and other strictly audible qualities of the note. You seem in addition to experience, even to hear, something about its temporal extent. (p. 208, 1)

Clark and Kelly are right to think this is a genuine phenomenon; I agree with Clark moreover that Kelly's description of the phenomenon is phenomenologically true to the facts. He gets it right. When you hear the singer's sustained note, you not only hear the way it sounds *now*, but you also hear it as having temporal extent. The note you hear *sounds* as if it has been going on for a while; it has that quality. This sets the stage for Clark's challenge. He writes:

> [T]he case poses a prima facie challenge [to the "presence-as-skill-based-access" approach]. If the perceptual experience depicts the sound as, in some real sense, right now (this instant) sounding "as if it has been going on for a long time", then this is one case where we cannot, even in principle, unpack that aspect of the phenomenology by invoking

capacities of access or exploration. For that which makes the note long is all in the past (we can assume it is ending right now) and simply cannot be "present to perception as accessible." (2006, 93)

The argument is pointed. One cannot explain the perceptual sense of the presence now of musical episodes that have elapsed in time by means of access to those episodes (sensorimotor or otherwise), for the episodes are over, past, done with, *inaccessible*. But then, Clark can be read as asking, what is left of the idea that sensorimotor skills play a constitutive role in making the world present in experience?

Clark is right that we can't understand the way in which the past is present in our current experience in terms of skill-based access, but this is no skin off the actionist, sensorimotor approach. For the actionist approach is not committed to any such account. To see why, consider that what motivates the skill-based access account of the perceptual presence of hidden parts of things we see is the phenomenology itself. *That's what it feels like.* It certainly doesn't feel as if you can *see* the back of the tomato, or that you merely think it is there. It feels as if you can *almost* see it, as if it is there to be seen, as if you know how to bring it into view. These are all things you can be wrong about, of course. But fallibility is not what's at issue. What's at issue is the character of the perceptual presence of the partially hidden parts of the things you see.

The phenomenology of the would-be presence-in-absence of the already elapsed portions of the sustained note is altogether different. Simply stated, there is not even a first-blush sense in which the elapsed sounds seem to be going on now. There is a sense that you can now hear the temporal extent of the sustained note. But it rides roughshod over the phenomenology of this phenomenon to say that the past sounds are *now present* or that they are now accessible. What is present to you now is the note you now hear. It mischaracterizes this phenomenon to say that it now sounds to you as if the past-portions of the note are audibly present, to say that you now have access to them. What needs to be explained is not the apparent presence of genuinely absent sounds. Rather, what needs to be explained is that the note you now hear *sounds* as if it has been going on for a long time. That is, what we need is a way of accounting for the perceptible quality of *temporal extent* without supposing, incoherently, that the past is present now, or that we now have access to what has already happened. It begs the issue and distorts the phenomenology to think that this is a matter of the qualitative presence of now elapsed sounds.

A clue to the needed account: the difference between objects and events. Objects, as already noted, are timeless in the sense that they exist whole and complete at a moment of time. Objects have no temporal extent. Events, in contrast, are creatures of time. They are temporally extended in nature. They are never whole. At the beginning, they have not yet achieved a conclusion. At the end, their beginning is done with. To suppose that the beginning of an event would be available, and so present, at its conclusion, in the way that the rear of the tomato is present, would be to suppose, confusedly, that events were in fact object-like structures. This would be to obscure the basic difference between objects and events.

Now back to the sustained note: Crucially, to perceive the note as sustained for a period of time is to experience something *happening*, it is to experience an *event*. It is not to experience something whose hidden parts are present but out of view. It is to experience something whose past and future parts are precisely *not present*. So it turns out that Kelly's question—*In what does our perception of the temporal extent of the sound consist?*—is in fact a special instance of the more general question, *How it is possible, at a moment in time, to experience an event, something which has no existence at a moment in time?* Or more pointedly: *In what sense can an event, which is fleeting and partial, be present to experience at a moment in time?*

Fortunately, there is an answer ready to hand. You don't need access to past sounds to experience the sound event (the temporal extent of the sustained note). What you hear when you experience the temporal extent of the note are not the sounds that have already passed out of existence (any more than you *hear* the sounds that are yet to come). What you experience, rather, is, to a first approximation, the *rising* of the current sounds *out of the past*; you hear the current sounds as *surging forth* from the past. You hear them as a continuation. This is to say, moving on to a better approximation, you hear them as having a certain *trajectory* or *arc*, as unfolding in accordance with a definite law or pattern. It is not *the past* that is present in the current experience; rather, it is the trajectory or arc that is present now, and of course the arc describes the relation of what is now to what has already happened (and to what may still happen). In this way, what is present, strictly speaking, *refers to* or is *directed toward* what has happened and what will happen. Just as in a way the front of the tomato is directed toward the back—indicates the space where the back is to be found—so the present sound implicates a temporal structure by referring backwards and forwards in time.

Consider that there is no *sensation* or *physical magnitude* corresponding to the experienced presence of the back of the tomato. In the same way there is no sensation or physical magnitude corresponding to the presence of temporal extent. Kelly emphasized this in his original formulation. "What you hear no longer seems to be limited to the pitch, timbre, loudness and other strictly audible qualities of the note" (Kelly 2005, 2008). The temporal extent of the sound is not a feature of the acoustic signal. The *arc* of the sound, or of the event, is an *arc of meaning*. It is an *intentional arc* (to use Merleau-Ponty's term). When you hear the singer's sustained note, you do not experience the acoustical properties of the sound, anymore than you experience the acoustical properties of the words you hear when you understand speech. In the linguistic case, you hear meanings themselves, you hear *what is said*. In the case of the singer, what you actually hear is the singer herself, her voice, her vocal action—what she is doing. It is the fact that the singer is doing something, performing an action, that fixes the relevant temporal horizon and intentional arc. Not any old sequence of occurrences is an event in this sense; events are sequences with a *sense;* they unfold in a direction according to a rule. A dancer's movements, a baseball player's throw, a singer's song, a speaker's utterance—these are meaningful events; the past and future are not present in them, but they are implicated by them. The able perceiver appreciates this implication.

For mere sensory stimulation to rise to the level of experience of something happening, you must understand the significance of that stimulation. Your perceptual *achievement* depends on background knowledge. The actionist, sensorimotor approach emphasizes *sensorimotor* knowledge. This knowledge is fundamental, I think. But there is no sharp line to be drawn between implicit understanding of the sensory effects of movement (sensorimotor knowledge) and other forms of knowledge that get drawn on in experience, as I argue in *Action in Perception* (Noë 2004). Consider the case of language. Insofar as we *hear* language, or *see it,* then linguistic perception depends on our possession of auditory and visual sensorimotor skills. It is the distinctive character of these skills that in part explains the difference between seeing and hearing (O'Regan and Noë 2001; Noë 2004). But the deployment of these skills is not alone sufficient for linguistic comprehension. Linguistic understanding is also required, as is a wealth of relevant cultural and contextual knowledge.

One consequence of this to which Clark (2006) draws attention is that, to a first approximation, *there are no new experiences* (a claim explicitly defended in Noë 2004). Clark writes:

> For there is a general puzzle, for [sensorimotor] accounts, concerning first time or genuinely novel experiences. In such cases there seems to be no background of sensorimotor understanding available to support (to constitute, on these accounts) the perceptual experience. But there seems to be no reason (apart from prior acceptance of the very model that the examples aim to call into question) to assume that we cannot experience a totally novel soundstream as structured, or a novel shape as shaped, or a novel taste as tasting thus-and-so, and so on. (2006, p. 24)

The impossibility of genuinely novel experiences is not a dogmatic consequence of the theory, but a discovery for which there is independent support. A strong case is that of language. Unless you know a language, it is difficult, maybe impossible, even to *hear* the relevant speech sounds. A truly foreign language is very noisy. Not so noisy as to prevent one from identifying it as *language*, but far too noisy to enable one to hear where one word stops and another begins, say. It is only against the background of familiarity that it is possible to experience language properly. Another strong case, consider the long-term blind who have undergone cataract surgery to restore sight (Noë 2004). It is well known that the surgery restores normal patterns of visual stimulation but does not yet enable normal visual experience, for the latter depends on further understanding of sensory stimulation.

We can bring out the way in which experience is possible only in a setting of familiarity, by the everyday example of listening to music for the first time, even music in a genre with which you are familiar. You play a record through. The music is unfamiliar, strange; the album exhibits a kind of opacity. As you become familiar with the music, you begin more fully to experience it. Your experience becomes richer. Where the songs were thin and meaningless before, they are now structured, complex, and motivated. Without acquaintance with the music itself, you were, in effect, unable to hear it. We can see this same phenomenon at work, but in a more extreme form, when what is at stake are radically unfamiliar musical styles. Many people find the music of other cultures barely counts as music; and it is common for people to describe experimental, "new music" as mere noise.

Schubert is said to have claimed: "It is easy to write a good song. You choose a melody that everybody recognizes but that no one has ever heard before." He understands the basic fact that we can only expand our experiential repertoire piecemeal, by nudging forward holding hands with what is familiar. For the most part, we are simply incapable of new sights, new sounds, new experiences. What we can perceive is limited to what we understand. This is not to deny Clark's claim that he experienced the train's lonesome whistle the first time he heard it, but it is to remind us that that experience took place in a setting of background understanding (sensorimotor and otherwise). What he heard, after all, was not just a sound, but *a whistle*, that is, the sound of the train as it whooshed by in the night.

This brings us to a question that lingers unanswered. Does the account sketched here of the perceptual presence of events conform to a skill-based *access* account? That is, can we say, in this sort of case, that one's sense of the presence of the event is a sense of one's skill-based access to the event? Yes. But we need to be very careful in our formulation of *what* we thus gain access to. When you experience the singer's song, it is the singer herself, as we have noticed, that you hear. Likewise, when you hear the train's lonesome whistle sound, it is the speeding train to which you thus gain access. Perception is an activity of sensorimotor coupling *with the environment*. It is not a type of engagement with mere appearances or qualia. When you attend to the sustained note, what you are thus able to establish contact with is the singer's continuous action of holding the note. The singer and what she's doing are available to you thanks to your situation and your skillful access. (This may be related to a more fundamental fact: that *objects* are primary in our experience; that experience of events depends on a more basic sensitivity to the presence of objects.)

For philosophers there may be a temptation to think of experiences as a kind of logical act, comparable to an act of judgment or to assertion. We find it natural to think of experiences as representations. But experiences are not acts, in this sense; they are not representations; they are *activities*, events themselves; they are temporally extended patterns of skillful engagement. When you perceive an event unfolding, it is not as if you occupy a dimensionless point of observation. You *live through* an event by coupling with it. What you experience is the event, as it plays out in time. You experience the singer's song, and the ball player's play, and the dancer's dance, by tracking what they do over time. The very experience is a world-involving achievement of control and attention.

5

✳

Presence in Pictures

"But this surely isn't *seeing!*"
"But this surely *is* seeing!"
—It must be possible to give both remarks
a conceptual justification.

—Ludwig Wittgenstein[1]

Introduction to the Problem

MY TOPIC is *seeing pictures*. Pictures are a central problem for the study of perception and consciousness, both in philosophy and also in psychology and cognitive science. One reason for this is that ideas about pictures have tended to shape the way theorists think about vision. To see, it is widely supposed, is to have picture-like representations of the world in consciousness; seeing is having a kind of mental picture. Vision in turn is thought to be the process whereby this kind of richly detailed internal conscious picture is produced. And of course, it is supposed to be produced from pictures in the eyes, *retinal* pictures. In my view, seeing is pictorial in none of these ways. Seeing is not a process that starts from retinal pictures—indeed, there are no retinal *pictures*—and seeing is not itself pictorial. Clearing up these misunderstandings about pictures is necessary if we are to find our way to a better understanding of seeing itself. Another reason the problem of pictures is central for an account of perception is that, as I will try to convince you, seeing pictures is not merely a way of seeing a particular kind of thing , namely, a picture (a photograph, a drawing, a painting, or whatever). It is, rather, *a distinct style of seeing*. Indeed, it would not be entirely misleading

---

1. This remark occurs on page 203 of Anscombe's edition of Wittgenstein's *Philosophical Investigations,* as part of the material she dubbed *Philosophical Investigations: Part II* (1953). Hacker and Schulte, in their new revised fourth edition, have reorganized and renamed this material. The cited remark now occurs as §181 of their Part 2, which they call *Philosophical Psychology—A Fragment* (2009).

to say that pictorial seeing is a distinct modality of perceptual consciousness. And so it is a test of the adequacy of any theory of perception that it provides the resources to explain, or that, at least, it is consistent with the explanation of, pictures and our experience of them.

The basic question I want to address is easily formulated: What do you see when you look at a picture? What do you see, for example, when you look at a photograph of a loved one, or at an image in the newspaper of the president? What do you see when you look at a painting of Jesus, or at a drawing of a building?

Although the question is easily posed, the phenomenon of seeing pictures is difficult to understand, both for philosophy and for science. Part of what makes the whole issue so tricky is that we can answer the question—*What do you see when you see a picture?*—in two different, plausible, but apparently incompatible ways.

On the one hand, when you look at a photograph of Hillary Clinton, say, you see *her.* After all, there she is, in the picture. This is not to deny that you also see the picture itself, that is, the physical piece of paper, or projection of lights on the wall, or even to deny that you see Hillary Clinton *by* seeing the picture thing itself. But it is to deny that that is *all* that you see. Every picture has a double aspect: it is there for you, as a tangible, physical thing, *and* as a presentation of (in our example) Hillary Clinton.

Suppose you were to say: "Well, I see a bit of paper with smudges of color on it and I interpret this as representing something I independently know to be Hillary." If you were to say this you would be utterly untrue to the character of your visual experience. You would be misdescribing what you see. We can bring this out in two different ways. First, any description of what is there that confined itself to properties of the physical thing, the paper and ink, or the projection of lights, would leave something out. It would leave out the fact that Hillary Clinton, or a human figure, shows up, that is to say, *pops out* for you, in the picture. Second, when you see Hillary in the picture, you are exercising your perceptual sensitivity to Hillary, or, as the case might be, to human beings. Only blindness, or a serious cognitive deficit, could prevent you from discerning this person in the picture. (This is why we can teach a child what a goat looks like, indeed, what goats are, by showing him or her pictures of goats. If the child is put together right, cognitively speaking, he or she will be able to recognize a goat when she meets one in person.)

So, Hillary confronts you when you see her picture. Hillary shows up for you, in your experience of the picture. She is present for you, visually, in the picture. Full stop. This is phenomenological bedrock.

On the other hand—critically there is an "on the other hand"—there is an obvious and undeniable sense in which you do not see Hillary Clinton when you see her picture. After all, she isn't there! There is more to seeing someone than learning what he or she looks like by visual exploration. To see something, in normal circumstances, is to encounter it. To see something, you must be with it in a shared space. Seeing is situational; it is a meeting. Indeed, it is tempting to put the point this way: seeing is not mere depiction.

We can bring out this situational aspect of seeing by reminding ourselves that seeing informs us how things are around us, but it also always informs us of our relation to things around us. We see *what there is*, but we see what there is *from here*, that is, from a vantage point or perspective. Perceptual awareness of an object is thus highly sensitive not only to changes in the object, but also to changes in one's relation to the object, changes brought about, for example, by movement. Consider: as you approach an object, it looms in your visual field; as you move around it, its profile changes. It belongs to the normal perceptual encounter with the thing that your perceptual relation to the thing is modulated and governed by movement.

But all this points to the fact that your relation to Hillary in the picture is not a perceptual one, at least not in the normal sense. How Hillary shows up in the picture is immune, after all, to the effects of movement-produced changes in your actual spatial relation to Clinton herself. Of course, how Hillary shows up in the picture is also insensitive to changes in Hillary herself. Just as seeing Hillary Clinton is one thing, and seeing her identical twin is another, whether I can distinguish them or not, so seeing Hillary Clinton is one thing and seeing her photograph is another.

Now, what I am calling the phenomenon of *pictorial presence*, or *presence in pictures*, only comes sharply into focus when we allow that both sides on this apparent standoff—"this is seeing!" / "this is not seeing!"—are in a way right. Hillary does show up for you when you see her in the picture, but she shows up precisely as—obviously, palpably, manifestly—*not* present. Critically, it is a natural and normal feature of pictures that they are not deceptive or illusory. When you see the picture, it does not look to you as if Hillary Clinton is standing there in front of you. (Although it is an interesting fact that some children, but not all, spontaneously reach out to pick things up *in pictures*.) It looks to you rather as if you see Hillary without actually being able to see her, you see her despite the fact that she is manifestly *not* standing there in front of you. And yet it is not as if the picture merely gives you a free-floating consciousness of Hillary, as it were outside of space and time, rather the way Dorothy or Auntie Em show up in the witch's crystal ball in *The Wizard of Oz*. Hillary shows up for you, in relation to you; she is present in the picture; but she is present—and this is the key— precisely *as absent.*

Indeed, I would venture to say that it is just this fact of the presence-as-absence structure of pictures that explains their remarkable, somehow fundamental power, what has been called their *Lebendigkeit.*[2] Ask the question, why do pictures matter to us as they do? Why do they move us as they do? A natural reply would be that pictures matter to us because that which they depict matters to us. A picture of Jesus is important to us, let's say, because Jesus is important to us. A picture of my mother matters to me because my mother matters to me. But this can't be the whole story. If it were, then we'd have no understanding of what the distinctive importance of pictures consists of; they'd simply be a kind of transparency. But a picture of my mother is important to me in ways that every episode of seeing her is not. And sometimes our attention is captured by pictures whose objects simply do not matter to us. (Van Gogh's peasant's shoes, for example; the shoes themselves do not matter to us. This example is famously taken up by Heidegger in his essay on the origin of the work of art.)

Pictures enable us to undergo a visual sense of the presence of something in its manifest absence. This is the key to understanding why they fascinate us as they do, why they are important in the ways that they are. My mother is in New York. I can't see her now. And yet she shows up for me in the picture. What gives seeing something in a picture its particular quality is that it enables you to perceive something—something perhaps very important, perhaps not so very important—which is otherwise

---

2. Horst Bredekamp develops this idea that pictures are "lebendig" (lively, living) in his *Theorie des Bildakts* (2010). I use the German to signal his striking, and maybe problematic, usage.

unavailable to you through ordinary perceptual channels. It is the distinct presence/absence dynamic of pictures that explains why every picture is, at least to some degree, a voyeuristic opportunity. And it explains something of the emotional *charge* and sharp fascination that pictures have for us.

The problem of seeing pictures, or the problem of presence in pictures—the topic of this essay—is to understand how this works. Pictures have a distinct presence-in-absence structure; they enable us to encounter the presence of what is in fact absent; they give us access to a world beyond our reach. And moreover, they give us a kind of sensual or perceptual access. *How do they do this?*

Psychological Approaches

Many scientists try to explain how pictures depict in a way that rides roughshod over the distinctive phenomenon of pictorial presence. A standard line of thought is that depiction is explained by the fact that pictures have special psychological powers. For example, it has been said that a line drawing represents what it does because the drawing itself resembles the psychologically real internal representation that would occur in us if we were looking at that of which the drawing is the drawing (see, for example, Hayes and Ross 1995).

This sort of account rides roughshod over the phenomenon because it relies on the idea that what makes seeing pictures of shoes a way of seeing shoes is that the state we are in when confronted with a picture of shoes is *exactly like,* or very similar to, the state we would be in if we were encountering the shoes themselves. This idea is embraced by some philosophers as well. Dominic Lopes, for example, endorses what he calls the mimesis thesis: "Pictures typically elicit experiences as of the scenes they depict, which experiences resemble, in important respects, face-to-face experiences of the same scenes" (2005, 12). He also says, "A person who sees O in a picture has an O-presenting experience, but she may also have an O-presenting experience by seeing O face-to-face" (2005, 24).

A problem with this proposal, it seems to me, is that if we suppose it is true, then we lose a grip on what makes the phenomenon of *pictorial presence* interesting in the first place. That is, it explains presence in pictures by explaining it away. What is remarkable, after all, about my visual experience of the peasant's shoes in van Gogh's painting—and here I repeat myself—is precisely the fact that it is an experience *of* something that is manifestly not there before me. The thing about pictures is that they afford us a visual sense of the presence of what is *visibly* absent. Pictures enable us to experience something plainly absent as, at least in a way, present. If the experience of the picture of the shoes were really like the experience of the shoes, this couldn't be what the presence in pictures was like.

We lose what is special about seeing in pictures if we adopt what Lopes (2005) calls *the mimesis thesis;* and so we also lose what is distinctive about *nonpictorial* seeing. To see a pair of shoes, in the flesh, is comparable to holding the shoes, or touching them. We see the shoes because we are *in situ* with them. In general, as I mentioned earlier, seeing is a mode of encounter with situations and things. It is a kind of entanglement. It is of the very essence of our visual experience of the shoes that the shoes themselves, in their very particularity, and in their determinate spatial relation to us, are involved. But that is just what is not the case when we are seeing the shoes *in a picture.* When you see the shoes in a picture it is of the very essence of the way the shoes show up for you that they are not there; they are presented in the picture as not there.

The upshot of this is that even if we allow, as I believe we should, that seeing something in a picture is a *bona fide* way of seeing it, we still need to insist that the *way* the object shows up as present in a picture is qualitatively different from the way it shows up in the flesh. And so it is a mistake to try to explain the power of pictures by appeal to a supposed sameness of these distinct *kinds* of experiences (pictorial and nonpictorial experiences).

This claim invites an objection: "Some pictures, some of the time, cause experiences phenomenally indistinguishable from experiences of their subjects in the flesh" (Lopes 2005, 45). This is precisely what we find with so-called *trompe-l'oiel.* One might argue that this fact alone shows that pictures are or at least can be in the business of eliciting just the sort of scene-presenting experiences that could be caused by the scenes themselves. One who makes this argument might admit that it isn't the case that all pictures are (to use the phrase that Lopes adopts, following the practice of others) *illusionistic* in this way; for example, it might be acknowledged that frequently pictures represent objects as having properties we would never experience them as having were we to see them in the flesh. It might also be allowed that even so-called il-lusionistic pictures—pictures that only represent objects as possessing features we would experience them as having if we were to see them— tend not actually to fool us, for the simple reason that when we see them, we not only enjoy experiences like those that would be produced by the scenes that they depict, were we to encounter them in the flesh, but we also encounter, say, their properties as pictures (e.g. the flat sur-face of the canvas, the frame, etc.) . What Lopes would seem to be com-mitted to is not that, as a matter of fact, pictures must always deliver experiences phenomenally indistinguishable from the experiences we would get from a face-to-face encounter with things, in order for them to have representational powers, but that the possibility of their so do-ing is, if you like, the limit to which pictures approach. Pictures that fool the eye, in this view, are the limit case; the perfect picture. Ac-cording to this way of thinking, there is one a single species of visual experience—the scene-presenting experience—which is enjoyed when we look at things face-to-face, and also when we look at pictures of those things.

If I am right, this reasoning betrays a blindness to the phenomenon of presence in pictures that is what makes pictures interesting in the first place. To be taken in by trompe-l'oiel is doubly to fail to see what is present—for insofar as you are the victim of the trompe-l'oeil, you are seeing a picture, and don't know that you are, and you are not seeing an object that you think you are seeing. In such a case, you are neither in the state of seeing what is, or would be, present in a picture, nor are you in the state that you would be in were you seeing what is depicted. And critically, you fail to have any pictorial experience whatsoever, for you fail to encounter the double-aspect, presence/absence dynamic that is characteristic of seeing in pictures.[3]

I grant that a trompe-l'oiel is a picture. But the delusory experience of such a picture is, at best, an outlying, limiting case of what it is to see a picture; we cannot generalize from it.

---

3. Wollheim (1990) emphasized that seeing-in is a basic psychological phenomenon ex-ploited by pictures. You can see a figure in a cloud formation. Not everything you see *in* something else is depicted. Pictures exploit our abilities to see-in for their own purposes. I don't endorse Wollheim's view, but he deserves credit for recognizing the double aspect of picture seeing.

A Neuropsychological Approach

The mimesis thesis, I have argued, fails to provide an account of seeing pictures because it relies on an insufficiently sensitive account of normal seeing. Any account of how we manage to see something in a picture needs to keep control of the fact that seeing something in a picture is not like seeing it in the flesh. Seeing in pictures and seeing in the flesh are, in critical respects, different *kinds* of experience. In his recent book, Mohan Matthen (2005) offers an account of picture seeing that preserves the basic commitment of the mimesis thesis—roughly, that seeing a thing and seeing its picture is an experience of the same basic kind—without losing hold of the apparent differences between seeing and picture seeing.

Matthen's proposal is that visual experiences have two aspects. They have what I will call, somewhat tendentiously, a pictorial content. And they also have what Matthen calls a "feeling of presence." The idea is that you can factor normal visual experience into a pictorial content and a feeling of presence. Crucially, these factors can come apart. In Matthen's view, the experience of *seeing*, say, a phone to the right of a lamp, and the experience of *visually imagining* a phone to the right of a lamp, agree in their pictorial, representational content, but they disagree in respect of presence. You do not have the feeling of presence when you merely imagine the couch, or when you imagine that there is a phone to the right of the lamp.

In developing this proposal, Matthen draws heavily on an idea that has been influential in recent visual neuroscience, namely, the idea that there are two distinct visual capacities, one for visual representation or experience and one for visually guided action, and that these two distinct capacities are supported by distinct anatomical structures. According to what is now known as the two-visual-systems hypothesis, vision for representation and vision for action can be doubly dissociated depending on the anatomical location of a lesion.[4] Lesions in the dorsal stream (that is, along a pathway from the primary visual cortex to the posterior parietal cortex) impair one's ability to use what one sees to

---

4. Milner and Goodale (1995) is the critical source of this version of the two-visual-systems hypothesis, although the view has important antecedents (see, e.g. Ungeleider and Mishkin (1982). For critical discussion of the view, see Noë (2011).

guide action (optic ataxia), whereas lesions in the ventral stream (from the primary visual cortex to the infertemporal cortex) impair one's ability to form a coherent picture of the visual world (visual agnosia).

Matthen's proposal about pictures, then, is this. A picture engages the ventral, seeing-for-representing system, but it fails to engage the dorsal, vision-for-action system. Pictures in effect induce a kind of optic ataxia: the scene shows up as depicted in your visual consciousness, but without any sense of its presence, of its being within reach. In this way, Matthen tries to have it both ways. When you see a picture of a scene, you enjoy just the representational, pictorial content that you would enjoy if you were seeing it, as the mimesis thesis would have it. And this explains why seeing a picture is in relevant respects a way of seeing what is depicted. But the account does not ride roughshod over the distinction between seeing and picture seeing, for the account offers a principled distinction between picture seeing and normal seeing. In the case of normal seeing, but not picture seeing, there is a feeling of nondescriptive, nonpictorial presence owing to the engagement of the dorsal vision-for-action stream. In Matthen's view, the power of pictures stems from their remarkable psychological properties.

This is an intriguing and in many ways promising proposal. I want to indicate three general reasons for dissatisfaction with it.

First, I am skeptical that we can dissociate visual experience into a pictorial representation plus a feeling of presence. For one thing, although the neuropsychological literature is full of remarkable perceptual deficits arising from brain damage, including, in particular, people who are unable to use the spatial properties of what they see to guide their own movements, I am aware of no cases in which perceivers report a sense of the world showing up for them as visually represented but lacking in presence or thereness.

Second, and related, dorsal lesions resulting in optic ataxia do not in fact have the effect of rendering visual experience picture-like. In fact, many dorsal patients are perfectly able to use what they see to guide action and are not in any way aware that they suffer a deficit in the first place.

Third, it turns out that the neuropsychological data don't support the two-visual-systems hypothesis (see Noë 2011). Or rather, they don't support the existence of anything like a general dissociation between vision for action and visual consciousness. Visual consciousness itself is always already an awareness not merely of, for example, *a phone to the left of a lamp*, but of particular items standing in definite, experienced relations *to oneself*, and so it is always, already, an *action-sensitive awareness of how things are*. If this is right, then the problem of presence (in Matthen's sense) must already be in place even if we are to account for so-called *ventral* seeing, that is, for the ability to learn, from looking, how things are.

At bottom, Matthen and other defenders of the mimesis thesis seem to take for granted that visual experience is unproblematically pictorial, as if seeing were, whatever else it is, a state of having detached, object-centered, pictures of the scene, in one's mind. In my view, this is an untenable conception of perceptual experience. I turn now to a more complete examination of this issue.

The Snapshot Conception and Presence as Access

The mimesis thesis—in the different versions we have encountered it—psychologizes picture seeing. Steven Pinker captures this psychologizing commitment perfectly when he writes, in a book that is rather misleadingly titled *How the Mind Works*, "Whatever assumptions impel the brain to see the world as the world and not as smeared pigment will impel it to see the painting as the world and not as smeared pigment" (1997, 217). Pinker's idea is that it is a fact about the causal powers of pictures that they trigger in us the very same sorts of effects that *would be* triggered by the world itself. The underlying motivation for this psychological account is the idea that visual experiences (or percepts) are themselves a special sort of mental or neural picture. Seeing Hillary Clinton, or the setting sun, or a couch, or a phone to the left of a lamp, is like having a representation of all that detail in one's head.

Indeed, what I call the Snapshot Conception of Seeing is the starting point for a good deal of empirical work on vision (as I argued in *Action in Perception*; readers familiar with the discussion there might want to skip to the next section). According to this conception, to see is to undergo snapshot-like mental pictures of the scene before you. You open your eyes and you are given an experience which represents the scene—picture-like—in sharp focus and uniform detail from the center out to the periphery.

This snapshot conception of visual experience is neatly captured by Mach's famous drawing of the visual field (Mach 1886/1959). Mach's drawing is not meant to be a picture of the room, or even a picture of the room as seen from a particular point of view (reclining on a divan, with right eye shut, fixating a point straight ahead). Rather, it is meant to be a depiction of what the seeing of the room is like, a treatment of the visual experience itself. Mach's drawing represents visual experience as sharply focused, uniformly detailed, and high-resolution. The visible world is represented in consciousness in full detail as if in a picture.

Empirical investigation of the nature of vision takes its start from this snapshot conception. The puzzle visual theory faces is that of understanding how it is we come to enjoy such richly detailed snapshot-like visual experiences when, it is supposed, our actual direct contact with the world in the form of information on the retina is so limited. The limitations are familiar: there are two retinal images, not one, and they are distorted, tiny, and upside down. There is a so-called blind spot in each eye. The resolving power of the eye is limited and nonuniform; outside the high-resolution foveal region, the retina is nearly color-blind and its powers of discrimination are severely limited. On top of this, the eye is in nearly constant motion, saccading and microsaccading from point to point in the visual field three or four times a second. As a result of saccadic suppression, the data made available to the retina takes the form of a succession of alternating snapshots and greyouts.

How, on the basis of this fragmented and discontinuous information, are we able to enjoy the impression of seamless consciousness of an environment that is detailed, continuous, complex and high-resolution? This is the problem faced by visual theory.

The orthodox strategy is to suppose that the brain integrates information available in successive fixations into a stable, detailed internal model or representation or picture. This stable representation then serves as the substrate of the actual experience. According to this orthodox approach, vision just is the process whereby the patchy and fragmentary bits of information on the retina are transformed into the detailed stable representations underlying actual perceptual experience. This is what David Marr had in mind, I think, when he wrote that "vision is the process of discovering from images what is present in the world, and where it is" (Marr 1982, 3).

Now, in my work I have spent a fair bit of time criticizing this orthodox account of vision. Here I wish to make one critical point. There is very good reason to doubt that visual experience conforms to the Snapshot Conception. Visual experiences are not picture-like. This is important for our assessment of the project of vision science. If visual experiences are not picture-like, then, bluntly stated, vision science has been barking up the wrong tree. If we don't enjoy picture-like experiences, then we don't face the puzzle of understanding how the brain gives rise to such experiences. That's not a task the brain needs to perform.

Now, the claim that vision is not pictorial has two aspects. First, it certainly is not the case that when we see, the scene before us is represented in sharp focus and uniform detail all at once *in our conscious minds,* as it would be rendered, all at once, in a picture. I no more actively see all the detail that confronts me than I see the back of a tomato on the counter in front of me. It is not hard to demonstrate this. Consider, for example, the phenomenon of change blindness.[5] You are unable to tell what is changing in the image in front of you, even though the change is entirely open to view. Somehow, you don't see it. Of course, it is also not the case that you experience an absence or an indeterminacy in what you see. The scene is there. You have a perceptual sense of it. But crucially, you don't have a detailed encoding of the scene before you *in your consciousness.* If you did, then surely you would notice the changes, when they occurred. But you don't.

Of course you don't need to work in a psychology laboratory to appreciate that we don't carry a perfect, stable, detailed, internal model of what is before us in our consciousness. Perceivers are active. They are continuously peering, squinting, moving, looking around, probing the environment to get a better look at what is going on. This shows that *we,* ordinary perceivers, are not content to consult an internal representation of the world; we are interested in the world and are continuously active in trying to secure access to it.

This brings me to my second point: not only is it certain that we don't represent the environment in consciousness in a picture-like way, it is clear, on reflection, that it doesn't seem to us as if we do. Granted, we have a very definite visual sense of the presence of a detailed environment. However, it is wrong to suppose that it seems to us as if that detail is represented in our heads, in our consciousness all at once, in the way that detail might be inscribed all at once in a drawing. The detail seems to be "out there" in the world, not "in here" in my mind. It

---

5. For a discussion of this phenomenon, and its significance, see O'Regan and Noë (2001).

no more seems to me as if all the detail is represented in sharp focus in my consciousness *now* than it seems to me *now* that the hidden parts of things I see—like the back of a tomato on a counter before me, for example—are present in my visual consciousness. Yes, I have a visual sense of the presence of the tomato's back. But it's a sense of its presence in visual experience precisely as *unseen*. And so for my sense of the presence of environmental detail. It is all there for me, but it is not all there as seen. It is all there as available to me, as ready to be seen.

One way to bring this out is by observing that the phenomenon of presence-in-absence, a phenomenon that, in this chapter, I have mentioned only in connection with pictorial seeing, is in fact the hallmark of *all* perceptual consciousness. (Indeed, it may be the hallmark of *all* consciousness.)

Presence-in-absence is a basic perceptual phenomenon. The occluded portions of things we see show up in our experience, even though they are manifestly hidden or out of view. They are present as out of view or absent. Or consider a uniformly colored wall. You experience the presence of the wall's uniform hue even though differences in illumination cause the wall to vary in brightness across its surface. You see the constant color somehow beneath or behind or, better, *in* the variable apparent color of the wall. The wall's color is present, for you, rather the way the back of the tomato is, or the detail in the periphery of the visual field. It is present *as out of view; it is present as absent.* Or consider the shape of a circular plate. You visually encounter its circularity even though, from here, its circularity is hidden from view. The profile of the plate, seen from here, is elliptical. The circularity is present but it is absent, in the way that the color or the back of the tomato is absent. It is present, but absent.

In cognitive science and philosophy it is sometimes supposed that the moral to be taken home from this is that we *really* see much less than we naïvely think we do. The rest is inference. For example, I *see* the front of the tomato. But I merely infer or judge that the back of the tomato is present. I *think* the presence of the back of the tomato, but I don't actually see it.

The problem with this line of argument is that it misdescribes the way the back of the tomato, or the whole voluminous tomato shows up in my experience. (Here we may be reminded of the way the so-called mimesis thesis misdescribes our sense of presence in pictures.) Obvi-

ously I don't *see* the occluded parts of the things I see. They are manifestly hidden, occluded, out of view. But despite this fact, despite this
fact that they are hidden, I have a sense of their presence. And crucially,
the sense of their presence that I enjoy is manifestly *visual.* We have a
visual sense of the presence of the hidden parts of the things we see.
The tomato *looks* to have a back. It looks solidly three-dimensional. This
has to do with the essential fragility of presence.

What we need to recognize, then, is that we have here a *bona fide*
perceptual phenomenon. Presence-as-absence is *the* perceptual phenomenon and understanding it is *the problem* of perception.

For ease of exposition I have been talking as if we can distinguish
what is really present, for example, the front of the tomato, the apparent color of the wall, the plate's elliptical profile, and that which is present somehow as *unseen.* But I now want to impress on you that *all*
perceptual presence is presence as absence. Perceptual presence, as it
were, is virtual *all the way in.*

Consider the front of the tomato. You see it. But do you see *all* of it?
Is it all in your conscious all at once? I would suggest that if you look
carefully, you'll appreciate that you no more see *all* of the front of the
tomato than you see every side of the tomato at once.

Experience is fractal in this sense. In the large, in the small, no
experienced quality is so simple that it can be taken in all at once. The
world is structured and complex and it always outstrips what can be
taken in a glance.

How then can we understand the sense of perceptual presence of
what is hidden, occluded, out of reach? We can't use what is given to get
at what is hidden for, as I have urged, everything is hidden. The key is
access as I have stressed throughout this book. If we think of what is
visible in terms of projective geometry, then vision isn't confined to
the visible. We do not see what projects to a point (in the eye, or head).
We experience what is available from a place. And the ground of availability is our skillful ability to reach out and take hold of the world
before us.

The visual world shows up as present, but not in the sense of being
in my head, but the sense of being *there.* The basis for our sense of the
perceptual presence of the world is our possession of the skills needed
to reach out and, as it were, touch what interests us. The whole scene is
present for me because any element in the scene is but the flick of an

eye away. I have a sense, now, of detail in the periphery, even though, now, I am not looking at it, because *now* I stand in a definite physical, sensorimotor relation to it. I understand, implicitly, not only that movements of my body will bring me into contact with the items around me, but I understand how to do this. And it is this sensorimotor integration with my environment that is the explanation of the phenomenon of perceptual presence.

Visual consciousness is a matter of having the world within reach. I can sit here and pick up this glass. But I can also pick up that podium. I simply need to go over there. I can pick up that briefcase too. I just need to cross the room. There's no magic boundary that marks what is really in reach and what is not in reach. Armed with the right skills (and, for example, the right prosthesis, or the right tools, or the right knowledge), I am entitled to feel *in touch* with my mother in New York. Indeed, all I need to do is dial my phone now, and there she is. We stand in a skill-mediated relation with the world and it is these skill-mediated dimensions of access that define the scope of our awareness.

Models and Substitutes

The mind is not a container that gets filled up with pictures or representations. The world is present for consciousness; it is not depicted in consciousness. The world's presence is its availability—an availability that depends on the fact that we find ourselves in it and on our possession of the skills needed to explore it, investigate it, touch it. All perception is active and exploratory; understood correctly, it is, really, a kind of touch, a kind of skillful probing with our bodies. The character of our perceptual experience—what makes some of it visual, some of it auditory, and so on—is fixed by the different things we do to bring the world to hand, by the different batteries of skill we bring to bear in our active encounters. What we call sensory modalities are in essence *styles* of exploration.

Perceptual presence is availability; the world shows up for us as accessible. This now forms the background and starting point for my positive account of seeing pictures. Insofar as we *see* in pictures, or with them, then, this must be because pictures afford visual access, that is to say, access to the world in a visual style, using visual skills. How do they do this? The problem of presence in pictures—the problem that arises when we take seriously the question, what do we see when we look at a picture?—comes down to this: how do pictures enable visual access to the world beyond them?

Traditional approaches—and approaches in cognitive science for the most part fall under the heading "traditional approaches"—psychologize this phenomenon, as we have seen. That is, they suppose that the real issue is that of understanding the psychological *effects* of pictures, how pictures trigger responses in the visual system (or for that matter, how they trigger emotional or imaginative responses). But that is exactly the wrong question to ask. The question is not, or ought not to be, how does the picture affect me by, say, giving rise to a picture in my mind, or consciousness, or brain? (Indeed, that would be the wrong question to ask about normal seeing.) The question ought to be, how does the picture enable me to gain access to the world in the precise ways that it does? We explore the world with pictures; pictures don't make worlds in our heads. What is the nature of a picture—what relation does it bear to the world—such that my encounter with the picture can be, as it is, an encounter with the world?

I think I've figured this out. We can explore the world in pictures because pictures are able to go proxy for the world, to serve as its *representative*.

The basic idea is simple. If I want you to see my house, I can either bring you to my house, or I can bring my house to you. But if I can't bring my house to you, because it is too heavy, or because it is bolted into the earth, or because I can't afford to do that, then I can bring you a miniature, or copy, something that can *stand in* for the house, something that can serve as a substitute. Niceties aside, that's what pictures are. They are substitutes. A picture of a house is a kind of *ersatz* house. More precisely, it is a model.—I will try to explain.[6]

To help fix ideas, let me say something about models. There are many different kinds of models, and we put them to work for many different purposes. Architectural models, for example, sometimes function in the design process; they can serve as a kind of sketch of an idea,

---

6. The idea that pictures are substitutes is developed by Gombrich in his famous essay "Meditations on a Hobby Horse" in Gombrich (1963). I believed that I had come up with this idea on my own. One day I sat down to read Gombrich's essay in an old copy of the book that I happened to own. I was astonished to see the paper had been heavily annotated by me! I had been a rather young student at the time of the first reading.

as a way of trying an idea out. Sometimes a model is used to document an already existing building, or to show a client what a not-yet-constructed building would be like. Sometimes models are identical to that which they model, as for example, when a *new model* is presented at an automobile show, or when you visit a condominium and inspect a *model unit*. Maps are models; but with maps, as with the architectural models, it is critically important that the map *not* be identical to what it models; a map made to a one-to-one scale with the mapped domain would be useless for most of the purposes to which maps are put. Sometimes, as in the case of fashion models, the model is selected as a particularly excellent and so exemplary instance of the very same kind of thing that it models.

There are models in science, such as computational models of storm systems. A computational model of a storm is not a storm, although, if it is a good model, its behavior can tell us a lot about the behavior of a storm. But animal models in the biomedical sciences are typically living animals (or living animal kinds). The monkey serves as a model for the purposes of a study into the effects of a certain drug on the immune system, for example. And there are models like Watson and Crick's famous construction of a DNA molecule, a model that was able to clarify a whole host of puzzles about how the molecule might perform its hypothesized functions.

A particularly interesting case is that of models in mathematics. Again, there are different kinds of models here, and they are put to work for different purposes. Consider the case of geometry: It is a striking and basic fact about geometry that a single triangle, written with chalk on the blackboard, can stand in for all triangles conforming to a certain specification. When we perform a geometrical construction on the individual triangle, we establish a theorem that holds for all triangles of the relevant type, if it holds at all. We think of the individual triangle on the board as an instantiation of all and only those features that belong to the abstract category of the triangle itself.

But models can also be improvised and provisional. If I want to give you directions, I may find it useful to let a saltshaker stand for one landmark, say the Brandenburg Gate, while the pepper mill stands in for the Victory Column. This knife here is the Strasse des 17. Juni, and so on. I can show you how to get from the Brandenburg Gate to the Staatsoper, by presenting you with the spatial relation holding among the saltshaker, the pepper mill, and the knife. For certain purposes, this is a perfectly good model.

Common to all these different modeling practices is this: models are tools for thinking about or investigating or perceiving something other than the model itself. We explore the model in the service of exploring something else. And so we are able to explore something remote and difficult *by* studying the model. How exactly do we do this? What allows us in this way to view the triangle as *any and all* triangles, or *this balsa wood model* as revealing the properties of an unbuilt building? How is it that models enable us, as they do, to extend the reach of our powers of thought, understanding, experience?

Now, it's striking that when we consider an architectural model, for example, we don't find ourselves wondering how the model somehow manages to produce in a perceiver just the psychological effects that would be produced by a possible or actual building. We don't ask ourselves how the model manages, somehow, to transport the mind of the perceiver through space and time to a remote, perhaps no longer existent or even altogether nonactual building. We don't ask these questions because it is immediately clear that this has nothing to do with the function of modeling. If the model is a good one, it may very well serve to inform us of the character of a possible or actual building, and it may likewise have all manner of robust psychological (visual, kinaesthetic, emotional) effects on us. But these facts—the informativeness of the model and its psychological power—are *consequent* on the fact that it is a good model; they are not *constitutive* of its being one. It is *because* it is a good model that it has these effects. The point is, the model is not itself the *effect* of a building—as it were a reflection of or a projection from it. The model is not, *in this sense,* a *representation of* the building of which it is the model. Rather—and this is critical—the model is a substitute, or proxy, or stand-in, for the building. It is not a representation of it; it is, rather, its *representative.*

Or perhaps we should say that this is what it is for a model to represent—it is for it to be a representative, a stand-in or proxy. Crucially, a model can represent, *in this sense,* without being either a *reflection* of the reality it models or the cause or template for a further representation (or image or reflection or "experience") in the mind of the perceiver. We don't need to suppose that a model produces a mental representation or a mental model in order to depict. A model is something we use to stand in for something else. (I think it is safer not to use the word "representation" for this.)

Our question then, the fruitful question, becomes this: what licenses or authorizes a construction out of balsa wood or cardboard, to stick with this example, to perform the role of serving as a representative or stand-in for a possible or actual building? It is clear that it is not the construction's psychological power, or even the information that it carries, that authorizes it to serve as the building's representative. For as we have already considered, the psychological power only comes on the scene thanks to the fact that the model *is* a model.

If I am right that a model is, in effect, a substitute, then it will be the case that two kinds of factors control whether a given object is licensed to serve as a model. First, nothing is a good or fitting substitute for something else *simpliciter*. It is only relative to this or that purpose, that we can say that a given object is a fit stand-in for something else. Second, and the first point notwithstanding, whether or not a given thing will serve as a stand-in will depend on the intrinsic nature of that thing.

As for the first point, it should be clear that nothing is a model *in itself*. That is, being a model is not an intrinsic property of a construction. It is, rather, a use to which the construction is put. Thus, one and the same construction can serve as a model or as a dollhouse. And so, that something is a model is not something that can be "read off" of the thing itself. A saltshaker can serve, for certain purposes, as a model of the Brandenburg Gate.

But crucially—and this is the second point—whether something is in fact a fitting substitute, relative to certain purposes, can depend on its intrinsic properties. The actual makeup of my construction contributes to its ability to be put to work as a model. Consider my tabletop model with the saltshaker, pepper mill, and knife. It may suit my purpose well. The items are ready-to-hand, they are small and manipulable, and they are easily surveyable as a whole. And so it is easy for us to set up a correspondence between items in the model and items in the domain we wish to model so that we can, then, in Wittgenstein's phrase, think the model in its projective relation to the world.

We need to be careful, though, in weighing the role of intrinsic properties of a model in accounting for the work of models. It is a non-accidental feature of models that their elements stand in relations that can mirror the relations of that which they model. In Wittgenstein's phrase (although the idea is not original to him) models and what they model must share the same multiplicity as that which they model. That is, the model is only a model if its elements have the same possibilities of combination with other elements as we find in the domain of interest to us. A street map, for example, must have markings corresponding to every street in a town, or at least to every street of a given size.

But crucially, a street map, no less than the tabletop model, is something *we make*.[7] There are no ready-made models. We don't find the isomorphisms we need in nature. We set them up. We decide that the saltshaker is a basic element of the model, and that neither the salt within, nor the holes in the lid, nor the lid itself, have any significance in the map. We decide how to *think* the model in its projective relation to the world (in Wittgenstein's phrase); that can't be determined for us by the intrinsic properties of the model itself. At the same time, it is worth noting that not any old thing will offer itself as useful for any old modeling purposes. If what I need is a way of showing you where to meet at the Brandenburg Gate, under one archway and not another, I would do better to find something that, as a matter of physical fact, has a bit more structure than a saltshaker. And if I have at my disposal a knife and a ketchup bottle, it is probably understandable (although in no sense determined) that I'll use the bottle to stand for the Victory Column and the knife to do duty for the Strasse des 17. Juni.

What licenses this substitution of the bottle for the architectural landmark? We do, in light of the questions we are asking, the problems we are trying to solve, the interests we are pursuing. But once we settle on a projective relation, in the setting of our needs, then the model itself takes over and does real work for us. Now the *actual* physical spatial relations among the elements of the model—structural features that are there for us to inspect—can instantiate the very spatial properties in the domain that are of importance. The architect's model, or even my tabletop model of landmarks in Berlin Mitte, can actually instantiate, for example, the spatial properties of the planned building, or the center of Berlin. I can learn about Mitte by studying my saltshaker and pepper mill, because with my arrangement of these common tabletop

---

7. I am indebted to James Conant, David Finkelstein and Alexander Arteaga for illuminating conversation on the topic of this paragraph.

items, I have made for myself an alternate and indeed entirely self-standing Mitte. And so I can investigate Mitte, I can achieve access to Mitte, by exploring what I have made for myself on the tabletop. On the assumption, that is, that it is a good model.

What do you see when you look at an architect's model, or at the triangle on the blackboard? Well, this depends on when you look and what you are looking for. What do you see when you look at text on paper? Patterns of ink distributed across the surface? Letters? Words? Or a poem? You *can* literally see a poem, and also literally see the ink. It depends on what you are doing. And so with models. You can see Mitte itself, as you cast your eyes across the lunch table. Or you can see the debris of our lunch. Within the context of the modeling practice, you are entirely justified in treating the concrete stand-ins, as that for which they are stand-ins. The model affords an opportunity for extending the reach of your access and so your understanding and knowledge. This employment of models is at the heart of scientific practice; if I am right, it is an abiding feature of lives with pictures as well.

Pictures as Models

I now come to my central claim: A picture—a photograph, a painting, a drawing, but also a sculpture or relief, without respect to whether these are works of art—is, simply put, a kind of model. Depiction is a special variety of substitution.[8] A photograph affords you access to its subject—Hillary Clinton, say, or your grandfather—in the way that a model of the Brandenburg Gate, or an architect's model, affords you access to the Brandenburg Gate or the planned building, respectively. You see Hillary *in* her snapshot, because the snapshot functions, for you, or for us, as a stand-in.

This proposal comes up against a formidable objection at the very outset, which I will refer to as the Immediacy Objection. As I have been at pains to insist, there is no internal or intrinsic connection of model to that for which it goes substitute. As a consequence of this, models are, it might seem necessarily, constructions whose significance can only be conventional and must be learned. And certainly, many models and

---

8. As noted already, Gombrich made essentially this claim in his essay "Meditations on a Hobby Horse" (1963).

model-using practices are highly technical. It takes training, for example, to appreciate the character of a proposed building from its technical drawings, and many models—the computational models of scientists, for example—are utterly opaque to anyone without special training.

But the striking thing about pictures is that they do not seem at all like models in these ways. Pictures are, or at least seem to be, immediate in their significance. You don't need to learn to see a photograph of your mother. If you can see your mother, you can see and make sense of a photograph of your mother. There she is, in the picture. She just jumps out at you. No special training required. Nor is there any sense in which you need to make a choice to use the bit of paper (i.e. the picture thing) as a substitute for your mother in order for it somehow to assume mother status. Pictures have a kind of vivid, powerful immediacy. They are active; they seem to act on us. Models just seem to be the wrong kind of thing for pictures to be. Models are passive, they seem. They are specialist objects to be studied. We use models. But pictures, pictures live!

I answer this objection in two steps.

First, consider a so-called graphical user interface such as the Macintosh operating system. This is strikingly straightforward and easy to learn and use. Of course, this doesn't mean that it is not a highly sophisticated bit of technology and engineering. It's easy for us to use *because* it has been engineered precisely with our talents and inclinations in mind.[9] It's been designed with no other purpose in mind than that of being easy for us. Or put more informatively, it has been designed to be *obvious* or *transparent* to anyone with the particular knowledge and skills that that we already have, e.g. a grip on what a desktop is, and a filing cabinet.

Things are exactly the same with pictures. Pictures are not found; they are made; there's nothing *natural* about them. But they are made *for us,* that is to say, they are made with our particular perceptual and cognitive capacities in mind. They are made to be easy for us to make sense of. To use an evolutionary comparison, pictures have been selected for to be straightforwardly accessible to us just on the basis of our normal perceptual and cognitive capacities. If you can recognize Hillary in a crowd, then you have all the skills you need to recognize Hillary in a picture.

---

9. I adapt this point from Terrence Deacon (1997) who uses the example of user-friendly operating systems to shed light on the nature of language. I am indebted to his writing. His thinking in this area has influenced me.

But that's not because you don't need special skills to see Hillary in the picture. You do. You need to be able to recognize Hillary.

A picture then is a special kind of model. I will call it a *visual model*. To understand a visual model you need only be able to see and think in normal ways. No further specialized knowledge or skills is required. Like an architect's model, a picture is a construction that instantiates features of that on which it is patterned. In particular, a picture instantiates the look or appearance of a thing or situation. (And looks, as I argue in *Action in Perception*, are genuine, if relational, features of things.) And so it can serve, for certain purposes at least, as a substitute for that of which it is the picture. You can't hold hands with a picture; but you can caress it with your eyes. Our perceptual and cognitive skills make it easy and natural-seeming for us actually to take up an attitude toward a picture that it would be appropriate to take up to who or what is depicted. That is, we *regard* a picture *as* the one who is depicted. This is why it need not be superstitious to kiss the photograph of a loved one. Pictures have the power to affect us emotionally because that which they depict has such power. (But not only for that reason.) It is the way pictures are made—the way they are related to the wider world, the way they remake important parts of the world—that makes them, really, little worlds themselves for us to investigate.

What these considerations establish is that the apparent immediacy and transparency of pictures is, in fact, an illusion, itself an artifact of their engineering. We confuse excellence of engineering with naturalness and immediacy.

Pictures are products of engineering. They are models and models are, as we have already considered, tools for thinking about things.

This brings me to the second stage of reply to the "immediacy" objection we are now considering. A general fact about tools is that their utility is highly context-bound. In particular, their usefulness is relative to the background of our needs and capacities. Take a doorknob, for example. A simple bit of technology, yes, but one that presupposes a vast and remarkable social background. Doorknobs exist in the context of a whole form of life, a whole biology—the existence of doors, and buildings, and passages, the human body, the hand, and so on. A designer of doorknobs makes a simple artifact but he or she does so with an eye to its mesh with this larger cognitive and anthropological framework. When you walk up to a door, you don't stop to inspect the door-knob; you just go right through. Doorknobs don't puzzle us. They do not puzzle us just to the degree that we are able to take everything that they presuppose—the whole background practice—for granted. If that cultural practice were strange to us, if we didn't understand the human body or the fact that human beings live in buildings, if we were aliens from another planet, doorknobs would seem very strange and very puzzling indeed.

And so with pictures. The pictures in the morning newspaper or the family album strike us as self-evident and natural. It seems to us as if they are like transparencies through which we see the world. In fact, pictures are simply tokens we put to use in a familiar communication game. We are at home in the game and so the game seems natural.

I once played a game with friends. We showed each other photos of familiar objects and places in the house where we were gathered. The task was to recognize what was depicted. The fun consisted in realizing how very difficult it is to recognize *anything* out of context.

I offer this anecdote because it helps us see something critical about pictures and their significance for us. It was hard to recognize or see anything in these pictures, because we didn't know what they were trying to show us. We had no idea what the pictures were being used to accomplish.

Seeing a picture requires stage-setting, for a picture is a move or gesture in a communicative setting. A picture communicates something or shows something. Or rather: someone shows you something with a picture. To get a picture, to understand it, you must, in effect, grasp what someone aims to show you.

Most of the time the rhetorical stage-setting for our encounters with pictures is obvious and settled. Typically we experience pictures *in a context*. Looking at photos in the newspaper, or in the family photo album, or in advertising, it's usually clear what's going on.

Earlier I conceded that you don't need to learn to see your mother in a picture. If you can recognize your mother, you can recognize her in a picture. But we are now in a position to see that in fact this isn't quite right. To see a picture—actually, to see anything—requires a sensitivity to context. Pictures in particular function in a communicative or rhetorical context. If that context is abrogated, as in the game I described, or if the context is unfamiliar, because you are a child, then pictures lose their immediacy. They go blank. (This is an empirical claim; but one that is, for obvious reasons, not easy to test.)

The upshot is this: there is no *natural* or *intrinsic* connection between pictures and what they stand in for. Yes, we can say that a picture, say, resembles its subject, that the painting of Hillary is a good likeness, and so on. But it isn't resemblance that grounds the depiction relation. Resemblance is itself consequent on the context-bound, purpose-relative activity of using pictures to stand in for things.

The Particularity Problem

Pictures of people raise in a particularly sharp form a problem that already arises for models more generally. A picture of Hillary serves as a stand-in or substitute for Hillary. In good measure, what enables it to do that is the fact that the picture itself is a construction of Hillary's appearance; like Hillary herself, the picture instantiates aspects of her appearance. And so we can study Hillary's appearance by studying our pictorial model of it.

The problem in all this is that it would seem that Hillary herself is left out of the story. Hillary's appearance is modeled in the picture, not Hillary. Hillary's appearance is not unique to Hillary; in principle, at least, it is a property shared by all her Doppelgänger. And this is not an accidental feature of pictures of people. There is no reason to expect that there should be any intrinsic difference between a picture of Hillary and, say, a picture of an exact, molecule-for-molecule duplicate of her (to use an expression beloved of philosophers). But then, we can ask, in what sense is the picture really *of her*, that is, of her *in particular?* In what sense, that is, does this particular person, rather than her multiply instantiatable appearance, show up for us in the picture?

It's tempting to suppose that the answer to this lies in the simple fact that Hillary herself participated in the process of the making of the photograph. Certainly something only counts as a photograph of Hillary Clinton, or of the pope, or of a UFO, if these items actually played a causally ineliminable role in the production of the images. A photograph, in this sort of view, is a kind of imprinting of an individual herself. The picture is *of* whoever was involved, in the right sort of way, in the manufacture of the image. If the picture is in fact a snapshot of one of Hillary's Doppelgänger, then it is not a picture of Hillary, even if it looks just like her. In this way of thinking about pictures, they are causal structures, rather in the way that autographs are. Something counts as Daniel Barenboim's autograph only if it was produced by his actual hand.

It would be natural to extend this to painting as well. The imprinting process is less mechanical, less automated, where painting is concerned. But certainly there can be no doubt that a painter grapples directly with that which he or she is depicting. Interestingly, we say of the painter at work on a portrait that the sitter is his or her *model*. As if the to-be-depicted world is itself, from the painter's point of view, a model to aid in the production of his or her ersatz world.

In fact, this causal theory of depiction is exactly *half* right. The relevant photographic or painterly causal relation is sufficient, other things being equal, for depiction. The fact that Hillary, or the pope, enter into the causal chain in the way they do does indeed entail that the images at the end of this chain are images of Hillary or the pope. But this causal relation is not necessary. Not every image of Hillary or the pope requires that they participate in the image-making process in this way as, in Aristotle's term, one of the *efficient causes* of the image. To understand this, consider the case of a simple model again.

What makes the saltshaker a stand-in for the Brandenburg Gate, in my tabletop model, is the fact that I put it to use as such. I *select it* precisely to stand in for the Brandenburg Gate. Because of this fact, the Brandenburg Gate itself figures in a causal explanation of why the saltshaker now has the significance that it does. But the causal relation here is of a historical, narrative sort, rather than of the billiard-balls-knocking-together sort.

Or consider a more detailed statue-picture of the Brandenburg Gate such as the sort of souvenir model you might buy in shops along the streets near the monument. Such an object was manufactured precisely to serve as a model of the Brandenburg Gate. What explains the fact that the model can serve in this way as it does as a model of the Brandenburg Gate is the fact that it was selected with this purpose in mind. More specifically, we can say that the model exhibits the features that it does *because* the Brandenburg Gate itself has those features. Crucially, the real Brandenburg Gate enters into the historical explanation of why this model came to be as it is and why, therefore, this little statuette is, as it were, destined to play the role of stand-in, for certain purposes at least, of the Brandenburg Gate itself. There is a causal relation here, but not of the billiard-balls-knocking-together variety. Rather, it is a causal narrative.

It helps get a sense of what is going on here when we notice that there is an asymmetric dependence between models and that which they model. On reasonable assumptions, that is, if the modeled object had been different, then the model would have been different too. That is, any situation in which things had been different with the modeled thing would be a situation in which, on the assumption that the model is a good one, things would have been different with the model too. The model tracks the object. But you don't get dependence in the other way. If the model itself had been different, there is no reason to suppose that the thing modeled would have been different. That is, there is no sense in which the object tracks the model.

And so with pictures. What makes this a picture of Hillary, rather than a picture of one of her possible Doppelgänger, say, is the fact the picture was manufactured *to be* a picture of Hillary. Hillary figures in the historical, causal story of its origins. Now it just so happens that Hillary herself figures in the causal story of the origins of this particular image in the further, photographic way as well. But that is, as it were, an accident. Being used as an imprint is just one way in which an object can figure in the right sort of way in the causal history of an image. Even when the depicted person is not used as an actual imprint—as when we are painting, or as when the depicted person is a historical personage whose physical body is lost in the sands of time—something only counts as a picture of so and so if so and so figures in the history of the picture.

Now, there is a mistake lurking in the vicinity. It would be a mistake to say that what makes the picture a picture of Hillary Clinton in particular is the fact that it is the artist's *intention* to target Hillary in this way. Wollheim may make just this mistake.[10] You can see Henry VIII and the actor Charles Laughton in a single picture, he notes; but what makes it the case that the picture is a picture of the king but not the actor is the fact that the painter aimed to represent the king. This psychologistic manoeuver is, once again, half right. Aiming to represent

---

10. See his *Painting as an Art* (1990, Chapter 2).

Henry VIII may suffice to make this a picture of Henry VIII (at least other things being equal), for this is one way to ensure that Henry himself figures in the right sort of way in the history of the picture. And this explains also why there needn't always be a likeness between picture and person for the picture nevertheless to count as a picture of the person. But such an act of intention is not necessary. What makes the picture a picture of Henry VIII is the fact that the king figures in an explanation of why the picture has the features it does; the actor figures in no such explanation. The fact that the artist intended to model Henry VIII is but one way in which it can turn out that Henry VIII figured in a narrative of the picture's history. But it is not the only way. Indeed, we have already considered a natural kind of counterexample: images created by an automatic imprinting process, for example photography. The results of the photographic process yield an image of the imprinting object regardless of what was intended by the artist. I may intend to make a picture of Groucho, and I make a picture that appears to all the world to be a picture of Groucho. But if the person before the camera was Chico, dressed up as Groucho perhaps, not Groucho, then I have made a picture of Chico. Likewise, a picture of Hillary's twin isn't a picture of Hillary even if it is indiscriminable from a picture of Hillary.[11]

So what makes a model or a picture a model or picture *of* a particular individual is the fact that the particular individual enters into the explanation of why the model is as it is. This explanation is causal and historical. We see precisely this sort of narrative explanation—teleological explanation—at work in adaptationist biology. Consider: Mother Nature does not *intend* to enhance the moth's fitness by coloring its wings. Enhanced fitness is no sense the *goal* or target of this process. Nor is it the *prior* or *efficient* cause of the change in the color of the wings. Yet enhanced fitness figures prominently in any adequate explanation of

---

11. There are interesting complications here. Suppose I, an artist, use Laughton as my model precisely of the king because, after all, he looks the way I think the king looked. I draw Laughton to depict the king. Is the resulting picture a picture of Laughton? Or the king? I think we should say both, and for the kind of reason my account offers. But note also that there is something odd about saying that the picture is a picture of the two *at one and the same time*, as it were. It might almost be better to say that we can use one and the same picture-object now as a picture of one, and now as a picture of the other, rather as we can use the famous duck-rabbit drawing now as a picture of a rabbit, now as a picture of a duck, but not as a picture of both simultaneously.

why the moth's wings are colored as they are. Had the wing coloration failed to enhance fitness comparatively speaking, then that pattern of coloration would not have increased in frequency in the moth population. In just this sort of way, the Brandenburg Gate, Hillary Clinton, and Henry VIII figure in any plausible story of why the statue, the photo and the painting are as they are. These images were selected, as it were, to enable access to their corresponding objects.

Pictures and Mind

I have claimed that seeing pictures is a distinct modality of seeing. Pictures can allow us to see what we could not otherwise see because it is out of view or far away or no longer around; in this sense, they provide a distinct kind of access to the world. Pictures afford a kind of extended perception, just as models, quite generally, provide an extension of the domain of the thinkable.

Traditional perceptual psychology has been puzzled by pictures and models. To clarify their nature, as I have sought to do, is thus to make a contribution to perceptual psychology. Traditional approaches to perception have found it impossible to avoid thinking of vision as, precisely, a process whereby a model is made in our heads. What we experience, really, is our own internal model. But the appeal to an internal model is otiose. We are in the world and have the bodily and cognitive skills needed to explore it at will. Why build an internal model when the world can serve as its own model? We have the skills needed to explore it.

When we see in pictures, we really do see models, if my proposal is on the right track. But here the models are very much on the world side of the mind/world divide. We explore the world by exploring pictures. Pictures are, really, just a particular neighborhood.

I now turn, briefly, to a problem that has already been touched on in Chapter 2. We can depict what is not, or what is yet to be, just as we can depict what is or has been. The Garden of Eden, the Freedom Tower that will rise on the site of Ground Zero in New York, the destroyed but not forgotten World Trade Center towers themselves, and Hillary Clinton, all of these can show up in a picture. How is it possible in this way to depict what is not or what will never be, along with what was and what is? This is what we can call the problem of the intentionality of pictures.

In a way, as we noticed in the earlier discussion in Chapter 2, the question itself conceals a confusion. The power of a picture to depict a nonexistent building is or ought to be no more puzzling than the fact that an architect can construct a model to show how a building ought to look. Pictures and models are substitutes and something is only a more or less adequate substitute relative to our needs and our purposes. Our needs and our purposes in turn will reflect our relation to that which we wish to model. Our need of a proxy for a not-yet-constructed building is quite a different sort of need from that which leads us to model a famous monument; and the role in our lives of a photograph of a deceased loved one will be different from the role of a newspaper image of a well-known politician.

The real confusion in the vicinity here is the tendency to think that if Hillary Clinton, Henry VIII, and Moses, can all show up in a picture, then there must be some single way they show up, or some single kind of reference relation that the picture bears to these individuals in virtue of which they can show up in the picture. But *presence in pictures* is accessibility, and access always depends both on our relation to the world around us, this in turn being shaped not only by what there is, but by what we know and what we know how to do. When we have the skills needed to pick up what there is, then what there is can be *there* for us, that is, present. And so with pictures. A picture affords access when it bears, relative to our needs and interests, an appropriate relation (that of the model) to what it depicts, and when we ourselves stand in the right sort of relation—the right sort of *epistemic* and *practical* relation—to that which is depicted. The access the picture affords me to the person who shows up in the picture depends, in part, on whether I know who Hillary is and what Hillary looks like. Moreover, the access afforded by a picture is shaped by a broader background context. Other things being equal, we trust that when we see a person in a photograph, we see them as they actually were when the photograph was taken.

This background is utterly lacking when we turn to a painting of Henry VIII. None of us has ever set eyes on this British monarch himself. Our epistemic and social relation to him is much thinner. He's dead and gone and at most we can rely on more or less trustworthy historical documents, other paintings, etc. We do see the king in his portrait; he is made available to us. But it is an availability that is qualitatively different from that which characterizes our relation to Hillary in her snapshot.

And likewise for the picture of Moses, whose very existence is questionable. What kind of access can we possibly have to something that, for all we know, is nonexistent? It would seem, at best, that we can have only a highly problematic and questionable access, something that may, in the end, be little more than the illusion of access.

So to these different styles of access afforded by pictures there correspond different styles of presence in pictures. My relation to Hillary in a picture differs qualitatively from my relation to the British monarch or to Moses. There is no *one* way things show up in pictures. Indeed, as with presence in pictures, so with *perceptual presence* more generally. Just as there is no *one* way things show up in pictures, so there is no *one way* things show up in our perceptual lives, or in our thought, more generally. As I look out at you, I enjoy a sense of your perceptual presence, but I also enjoy a sense of the presence in my perceptual experience of the room next door. I don't *see* it, of course, but then I don't *see* each and every one of you. You, and the room next door, are both more or less ready to hand, more or less nearby, more or less remote. Each of you, and the room next door, occupy positions in a *space of access* that defines the extent of my perceptual awareness.

Presence is access; this has been our theme throughout. This is true of pictorial presence and perceptual presence; and, as we have considered in earlier chapters, it is also true of what we can call *presence to mind,* or intentional directedness, more generally. For something to be an object of thought or interest or worship or anxiety is for it to be more or less accessible to me, and in more or less different sorts of ways, that is, along various routes of access. No access, no presence. The foundation of a more general theory of intentionality, or intentional directedness, then, is the theory of skillful access. Some forms of access depend not only on sensorimotor skills but on conceptual and sociolinguistic skills and on the large-scale fabric of culture including its various artifacts and technologies of calculation, navigation, transportation, information storage and retrieval.

Can we think of what is not the case? It seems as if we can. After all, we can think about something—Moses, Henry VIII—in its absence, and so we can think about something when, for all we know, it might not or might never have existed, or so it seems. Philosophers have sometimes concluded that this shows that intentional directedness is not an actual relation holding between a thinker and an object. After all, if

I can worship a nonexistent god, then my attitude to the god cannot be an actual relation obtaining between me and the god, for there is no god.

But that is much too fast. There is no *one* relation—reference, as it were—between a thinker and an object that constitutes intentional directedness. The fact (if it is a fact) that when my thoughts turn to Moses, I am not participating in an actual Moses-involving relation, does not show that when my thoughts turn to Hillary, or this tomato, or my mother, that I am not participating in a Hillary, tomato or mother-involving relation. The world shows up for me in consciousness as available. We can think of ourselves as standing in a whole host of relations to what there is (or to what, for all we know, there is). The kind of presence to mind that things have for us reflects the more or less attenuated, more or less reliable, relations we bear to them. My consciousness of the thing in front of me is one thing. My consciousness of things very far away from me is qualitatively different. And when there is really *nothing* to which my thoughts are directed, then, really, there is no thinking *of* something going on at all. There is only the illusion of thinking of something. Intentional directedness is always skill-based access. This is something we can learn from our investigation of pictures.

6

✳

On Over-Intellectualizing the Intellect

The World Available from Here

ACCORDING to an old and tired idea, the scope of experience is fixed by what projects to our eyes, or to the sensory periphery of our bodies. Experience, then, is something that happens inside us as a result of our being so affected by the world around us. I reject this way of thinking about experience and its scope. We see much more than projects to the eyes. We experience what is hidden or occluded (the tomato's back, for example); we experience the nature of things (what they are—telephones, say, or other people); we perceive emotion and meaning (the intensity of a person's concentration; what she is saying).

Of course, there are constraints on what shows up for us in experience; and these constraints have to do with our physical, embodied, spatial relations to things. But it is impossible even to begin to make sense of what shows up in terms of a one-way causal influence of the things around us on our nervous system, as I have argued in *Out of Our Heads* (2010).

Instead of thinking of what we experience as fixed by the way the world projects to us, giving rise to events of consciousness inside of us, we should think of what is experienced as what is *available* to a person, as what is available to a person *from a place*. The seeing does not happen in the head. Rather, the experience is achieved or enacted by the person. We do it *in the world*. The scope of experience is a matter of what is available to us. And what is available to us depends on not only what there is, but also, crucially, on what we can do. What we can do depends in turn on understanding, know-how, but also on tools and technology (pictures, language, the telephone, the pencil), and on where we find ourselves and what environmental or social resources are available to us.

What is available is that to which we have access, and the ground of access is knowledge, understanding, and skill. Mere sensory projection is neither necessary nor sufficient. It is understanding that brings the world into focus for perceptual consciousness.

Transformations of the Understanding

One of reason why art matters to us, I think, is that it provides opportunities for us to recapitulate this basic fact about ourselves: understanding and skill enable us to bring the world into focus for perceptual consciousness.

Consider what sometimes happens when you encounter an unfamiliar art work. Every song on the new record (for example) may sound more or less the same, each coming across flat, or unengaging. Every painting in the gallery presents its face to you, but only as a face in a crowd, with no discernable features. Sometimes we encounter the work, but it is as if we don't see it, or can't see it, or don't see any meaning in what we see.

But suppose you don't give up. You listen to the record again and again; you begin to notice different qualities in the different songs. As you familiarize yourself with them, they begin to engage your attention, and offer you comfort, or excitement, or stimulation, or pleasure. Perhaps you discuss the music, or the paintings in the gallery, with a friend, and she draws your attention to patterns or devices or lyrics. Whereas before the works—the songs, the paintings—were flat, opaque, undifferentiated, now they reveal themselves to you as structured and meaningful, as deep and involving. Each song, or each painting, now shows you its very own distinctive face. You make its acquaintance.

If you have spent time around art, you have probably had this experience. To a child all "classical music" sounds the same, just as every white-haired figure presented in eighteenth-century garb "looks like" George Washington. We don't differentiate well among the unfamiliar; this partly explains why the rural Nigerian border guards thought my girlfriend and I looked so much alike that we must be brother and sister. Or consider the case of literacy: to an illiterate person, the text might as well be invisible. The consciousness of the person who can read, in contrast, is captured by the text and by all that it affords.

We gain knowledge, and familiarity, and skill, and so we are able to bring the world into focus for perceptual consciousness.

Empiricism and the Philosophy of Mind

Some philosophers think of perception as nonintentional and nonconceptual. These philosophers are empiricists. Empiricism holds that perception is basic in our cognitive lives. Perceptual experience, for empiricists, is prior to and independent of our ability to think and talk about objects. First we perceive, then we frame concepts so that we can represent what we perceive in thought and refer to what we perceive in speech. For empiricism, perceptual consciousness (awareness, experience—I use these interchangeably), does not depend on possession of concepts or knowledge of the reference of terms; it is what first makes the latter possible. Empiricism is realistic and it is foundationalistic. The basic constraint on what we can see is what there is; our perceptual sensitivity to objects and their basic properties such as size, shape and color is the foundation of our cognitive lives.

In this chapter, and in all my work, I advance an anti-empiricism that denies that perceptual experience is prior to thought and talk. I do not claim that we need to be able to think of things prior to our encounter with them in experience; what I urge is that the conditions for encountering a thing in experience are also conditions for encountering that very thing in thought. Perceptual experience can enable us to be aware of things only given the coinvolvement of understanding. Perception and thought arrive at the party together. Thought is not prior to experience; experience is itself a kind of thought. But then thought itself, as we have seen, at least sometimes, is a form of perceptual consciousness.[1]

---

1. Tyler Burge recommends that philosophy should take its lead from the psychology of vision which is, he writes, "an exceptionally advanced and scientifically sophisticated area of psychology." My own attitude to the science is somewhat less deferential; vision science tells us very little about visual experience and what it does tell us fails to be, as concerns

From the standpoint of empiricism, the conception of experience as thoughtful and active that I defend here over-intellectualizes experience. For to suppose that perceptual experience relies on the exercise of the understanding, as I do, might seem to threaten to treat perception as if it were judgment or categorization. Certainly it does not ring true to suggest that we see things, as it were neutrally, and then subsume them under concepts. Such a view would over-intellectualize perceptual experience, presenting seeing as if it were a kind of contemplative detachment.

What is sometimes unnoticed is that this line of criticism is itself guilty of an act of over-intellectualizing. But what is over-intellectualized, in this line of criticism, is the intellect itself—as if the only legitimate exercise of the understanding was in a deliberative act of bringing things under concepts. If we think of understanding that way—as the exercise of deliberative judgment—then it is hard to take seriously the idea that experience rests on the understanding in the way I have urged.

Nothing compels us to think of the understanding in this detached, deliberative way. We can find an alternative conception in Wittgenstein. For Wittgenstein, understanding is akin to an ability. Understanding a concept is having a skill. One way to exercise the relevant conceptual skills is in explicit deliberative judgment; but that is not the only way. There is a distinctively perceptual mode of exercise of intellectual and conceptual (and also sensorimotor) skills. This is nicely illustrated by the phenomenon of linguistic perception. When you know a language, you can perceive words, sentences, even meanings; when you don't know a language you are unable even to discriminate these linguistic objects. They are not existence dependent on your knowledge, but your knowledge—your fluent, skillful mastery—is a condition for them showing up for you.

---

the current context, in any way dispositive. I am willing to agree with Burge, within some reservations attaching to use of the word "representation," that science demonstrates that "lower animals [such as honeybees, frogs, goldfish, pigeons, octopi] exhibit perceptual constancies and discriminatory behavior that make it clear that their visual systems are representing features of the physical world, not simply reacting to stimulus frequencies, and not simply carrying information in the sense that tree-rings carry information" (2003, 515). But this provides no support for empiricism. It is odd, to be sure, to think of honeybees understanding what they see; but it is not odder than thinking of them as experiencing what they see. Anti-empiricism of the kind I defend here asserts that the problem of understanding and that of experience are, in effect, the same problem. In presenting this anti-empiricism, I take myself to be extending ideas of Kant, Strawson and McDowell.

Wittgenstein's (1953) discussion in *Philosophical Investigations*, especially the discussions of rule-following, elucidates the idea that understanding is like a practical skill. In particular, as I read Wittgenstein, he
discovered that it is psychologism to hold that my actions can be rule-
governed only if I explicitly entertain the governing rule in mind. Crucially, as Wittgenstein argued, following a rule is only one of the
different ways for rules to govern what we do. The novice uses the rule
as a draftsman uses a ruler; as an active guide. The expert no longer has
any need for such explicit reliance on the rule. He has learned how to
act in accordance with the rule without any need to consult the rule in
thought (even in unconscious thought). But that doesn't mean that the
behavior is no longer rule-governed. The expert's skill allows for fluency and automaticity, but the zone of fluency is not one where the
rules lose their force and relevance. The master acts in accord with the
rules without thinking of them deliberately precisely because he or she
has mastered them. We see this in the chess grand master whose play is
a free and spontaneous expression of understanding.

Making It Explicit If We Can

Hubert Dreyfus has a different conception (see, e.g. Dreyfus 2006). He
contrasts the detachment of thought and reason with the engagement
of what he calls absorbed coping. The novice is a thinker: detached, at-
tentive, conscious, deliberate. The expert is involved in the activity and
has left the conscious mind behind. The expert is in the groove; for the
expert, what matters is the flow. This analysis is supported by empirical
findings to the effect that the expert's performance is disrupted by focused attention on the execution of the task, whereas the performance
of a novice improves when attention is brought to bear in this way. For
Dreyfus, the assumption that the grand master's play flows from an
understanding of rules is a giveaway of a shaping idea that he has called
"the myth of the mental," the idea that engaged, skillful coping requires
the backing and support of robust, regulating cognition.

Dreyfus urges that grand masters, in the groove, don't make moves
for reasons. They just act, responsive to the demands of the situation.
Dreyfus is right about the immediate responsiveness of experts. But this
doesn't mean that there is no place for thought or reason in an account
of what the expert does. We can agree with Dreyfus that the fact that

the grand master is able to tell you why she acted, after the fact, no more shows that she acted from a reason than the fact that the refrigerator light is on whenever you look shows that it is always on (as Sean Kelly 2008 has remarked). But it would be a mistake to think that the question whether she acted for a reason depends on whether she entertained reasons (even unconsciously) before acting. That presupposition is tantamount to the psychologism that Wittgenstein warns against. What mastery (or understanding) of rules enables is for one's actions to involve the rules without needing to think about them in any explicit, deliberative way. Again, language is a good object of comparison. There are rules that govern our use of words. Our skillful linguistic behavior expresses our knowledge of these rules. But there is certainly no requirement that we consider the rules that would justify our usage while we are caught up in the stream of linguistic activity. And so with chess, and action more generally.

Nor does one's inability to make explicit the rule that would have justified one's move (or one's speech behavior) show that one's action was not the skillful expression of mastery of a rule. Perhaps I can say nothing more articulate about why I moved as I did than: "this is a weak pawn structure; in a case like this you need to try to strengthen your defenses," or some such. Dreyfus is inclined to say, of this sort of case, that it shows that understanding, reason, thought, have left the building; the player is responding to context, to situation, to the brute solicitations of the state of the board. But this reply ignores a better alternative: that it might be essential to our conceptual and intellectual skills, as it is essential to every other kind of skill, that their deployment be context-sensitive and situation-dependent. The fact that the chess master can't give a context-free, situation-independent statement of the principle that governed her action does not show that understanding and reason were not at work.

It is to over-intellectualize the workings of the intellect to suppose that every exercise of understanding requires a deliberate act of contemplation of an explicitly formulated rule. Such an over-intellectualized conception of the intellect leaves out the possibility that intellectual skills themselves may admit of expertise and effortless exercise. Dreyfus is right to attack what he has variously labeled cognitivism, rationalism, representationalism. But he aims his attack at the wrong aspect of these doctrines. They do not go astray because they cite rules, justifications, reasons, and understanding, in offering an account of action and experience. They go astray, rather, because they take for granted that the intellect's operation is always deliberate and detached. And this is Dreyfus's mistake as well. Like the views he attacks, Dreyfus takes for granted that there can be no operations of the intellect that belong, as it were, to the engaged mode. That's precisely the way of thinking about the intellect made available by Wittgenstein. Our understanding, our thinking, our deliberations themselves, always only take place in a context, against a background, and for certain purposes.

Awareness of What the World Affords

I turn now to a line of objection that has been leveled against the sort of conception of experience as skill-based access that I develop here; it has also been pressed against Gibson (1979). To bring the objection into view, recall that for Gibson affordances are the possibilities for action provided by things. A tree stump affords sitting; Gibson argued that we perceive affordances.[2]

The way traditional cognitive science understands this, the idea would be that we see the tree stump, say, and represent it as affording sitting.[3] In this way, perceiving the affordance is, in effect, an act of categorizing or classifying the tree. To see the tree's sit-upon-ability is, in effect, to bring the object under the concept of seat. It may not seem to us, when we see the tree's affordance property, that this is what we are doing. But phenomenology, it is observed, is not a reliable guide to cognitive psychology.

Gibson's own theory of affordances was advanced as an alternative to this perception-as-classification idea. This is what he had in mind when he said that we see affordances directly.

---

2. Gibson writes: "The different substances of the environment have different affordances for nutrition and for manufacture. The different objects of the environment have different affordances for manipulation. The other animals afford, above all, a rich and complex set of interactions, sexual, predatory, nurturing, fighting, playing, cooperating, and communicating. What other persons afford, comprises the whole realm of social significance for human beings. We pay the closest attention to the optical and acoustic information that specifies what the other person is, invites, threatens, and does" (1979, 128). It is worth underscoring the great generality of the affordance concept for Gibson. What a thing *is* (as well as what it *invites, threatens, does*) belong to its affordances.
3. See, for example, Fodor and Pylyshyn (1981).

It is usually supposed that there is something special about affordances, for Gibson, in virtue of which we can see them directly. And then the question is, what is it about the fact that a thing affords me the possibility of action that allows me to see it in a way that I could not otherwise see it. John Campbell has criticized Gibson on this sort of ground. Campbell writes,

> Suppose, for example, that an unfamiliar piece of apparatus appears on a workbench. I have no idea what this thing is for. I don't know if I can touch it—maybe I will be electrocuted, or the thing will blind me, if I do that. Or maybe it is simply the latest kind of television, or a paper weight. So I don't see it as affording anything in particular. In that case, by Gibson's theory, the thing should be simply invisible; I should be able to see it only when I am told what it is for. But that is not a persuasive conclusion; it seems perfectly obvious that we can see things without knowing what they can be used for. (2002, 43–44)

As I read Gibson he is not committed to such a conclusion, for it is not Gibson's view that we only see affordances, or that we can only see objects insofar as we can see their affordances. Gibson's point comes earlier: that we *can* see affordances. The significance of his thought is this: for Gibson, perceptual consciousness is not confined to so-called categorical (or categorial) properties of things, such as shape, say, or size, or qualities like color. Gibson is advancing "the radical hypothesis" that "the "values" and "meanings" of things in the environment can be directly perceived" (1979, 127).[4]

This is just what Campbell denies. As Campbell writes, the

> natural view to oppose to Gibson is that visual experience does not provide us with knowledge of affordances. It provides us with the knowledge of the categorical properties of objects which are the reasons why objects have the affordances they do. (2002, 44)

And he continues:

> This is particularly compelling when you consider shape properties . . . It surely is plausible that ordinary experience of the shape of an object

---

4. Gibson is clear that we do not only perceive affordances. For example, we perceive also the "composition and layout of surfaces." He writes: "Perhaps the composition and layout of surfaces *constitute* what they afford. If so, to perceive them is to perceive what they afford" (1979, 127).

does not provide you merely with the endless opportunities for various types of action made possible by its having that shape. It confronts you with the categorical shape property itself, the reason why the object provides all those properties. (2002, p. 144)[5]

As I interpret Campbell, his charge is that Gibson gets things backwards. We don't see things by seeing what they are for; we see things and so, on that basis, learn about what they are or might be for. A very similar line of criticism can be (and has been) framed against the sort of conception of perceptual experience as constituted in part by the exercise of what I have called "sensorimotor understanding" or "sensorimotor expectations" (that is, by expectations about the way sensory stimulation varies as a result of movement).[6] Sensorimotor expectations cannot be constitutive of perceptual awareness of an object, for it is the antecedent perception of an object, with its stable, independent nature, that gives rise to and justifies sensorimotor expectations in the first place, so the objection goes. My sense of how the appearance of something will change as I move is simply the wrong sort of thing to serve as the ground of my successful perceptual contact with the object itself. For how can a wealth of contingencies of this sort give one access to the underlying basis of those contingencies, to the object itself? And where do we even get the idea that the object is there independently of how we experience it?

I have already mentioned that it isn't Gibson's view that, as Campbell puts it, the experience of the shape of an object provides you "merely with the endless opportunities for various types of action." Nor is it my view that what we really experience are patterns of appearance and the way they change as a result of movement. Neither Gibson nor I wish to deny that ordinary experience is a confrontation with objects themselves. What I deny—I don't want to speak for Gibson here—is that we

---

5. Burge has something similar to say. "Insofar as there are perceptual representations of *danger* they are essentially associated with perceptual representations of types of shape, movement, and so on. They are commonly formed (perhaps innately) through grouping representations of properties that signal properties relevant to the animal's needs" (2003, 515).

6. Campbell (2008) himself develops this line of criticism in his contribution to the symposium on *Action in Perception* in *Philosophy and Phenomenological Research*. Christopher Peacocke and Benj Hellie have voiced this line of criticism to me in discussion.

can just take for granted the fact that objects and their so-called categorial properties show up in experience. It is our unavoidable perceptual predicament that there is no such thing as a perceptual encounter with the object that is not also an encounter with it from one or another point of view; there is no such thing as seeing an object from every point of view at once; so objects of perception always have hidden, nondisclosed parts or aspects. What I call the problem of perceptual presence is that of explaining how a merely perspectival glimpse of something can disclose its nature when that nature transcends what is contained in a single glimpse alone. In this chapter, and throughout this book, I have offered a solution: what enables us to achieve perceptual contact with objects despite the limited and partial character of our perceptual situation is our understanding (sensorimotor and otherwise). Sensory events alone, without skill and understanding, are blind.

Adjusting for the World's Presence

I suspect that Campbell and other empiricists suppose that affordances, or appearances, are not real, or at least, that they are not sufficiently basic. Animals perceive danger and sexual availability and opportunities for concealment, it would be admitted, but they do so thanks to a more basic ability to represent shapes and sizes and movements of things. There are two big and by now familiar problems with this line of response.

First, as already stated, we cannot take for granted our perceptual access to objects and their shape and size. The problem of perceptual presence—namely, the problem of what our perceptual sense of the presence of features that are manifestly out of view or hidden consists—arises for every perceptual object or quality whether we think of it as categorical or dispositional.

Second, the contrast between categorical and dispositional properties collapses. Among the things I can learn from what I see are how things are with respect to shape and size, but I can also find out about how things look. Indeed, it belongs to our perceptual predicament that in visual perception I must learn about how things are by looking and so by making sense of how things look. The empiricist tradition has tended to assume that looks are subjective dispositions of one kind or another. They are effects in us; matters of sensation. In an effort to break with what Putnam (1999) has called the interface conception of experience, it might seem that we need to do away with the idea that we are aware of looks (for example). But that is dogmatic and unreasonable. We need to rethink what looks and other appearances are. They are not "in here," and it is not our burden to get from them, somehow, to what is "out there." Nothing forces that interface conception on us. I have argued that appearances are environmental properties. If we want to think of them as dispositions, then they are the ways objects affect their environment, not ways they affect our sensations. Perception is an activity of learning about things by learning about how they affect the world.[7]

Similar remarks go for affordance properties. The grass can show up for me in perceptual consciousness as a place to rest; the animal can show up for me as a threat, or as a desirable mate. The fact that the perceiver's nature, and other environmental conditions, are factors determining what something affords me, does not mean that a thing's affordances are not among what I can directly perceive.

What enables us to bring objects into focus for perceptual consciousness, and also their affordance properties or other forms of significance, is our understanding (sensorimotor and otherwise). This is something that Gibson, no less than Campbell and (for rather different reasons) Dreyfus, seem to have been unwilling or unable to allow. Concepts and sensorimotor skills get applied in perceptual experience in the distinctively perceptual mode. That is, we don't use conceptual or sensorimotor rules to categorize objects or to represent them in our minds. Conceptual and sensorimotor skills are not means of representation; they are means of achieving access to things. Indeed, a theory of direct perception requires us to appreciate anew the role played by skills

---

7. Vision is an activity of learning how things are by learning how things look. This claim depends on thinking of looks as aspects of the environment to which we can be sensitive. I develop this account of looks in *Action in Perception* (Noë 2004, Chapters 3 and 4). None of this is to deny that there is also a way of talking about looks or other appearances ("looks talk") that serves a very different purposes, e.g. that of describing the character of one's percept in a way that withholds any implication about how things are, as when one tells the optician that the letters are blurry. One can give up the interface conception—as Hilary Putnam calls the idea that we are aware of something mental when we have visual experience—without denying that looks can be subjective in this sense. Putnam, Jim Conant and John McDowell have pressed this point in conversation in response to this chapter. This is an important topic for further investigation.

and understanding in perceptual experience. The object's nearby existence does not suffice to enable the object to show up for perceptual consciousness. To achieve contact with the object and its different kinds of properties requires skill—skills of a sensorimotor as well as intellectual variety. Conceptual skills, along with sensorimotor skills and other kinds of understanding, belong to the means by which we accomplish perceptual contact with reality. In perceptual application, we don't use concepts to represent things in thought, or to categorize; concepts are part of the adjustments whereby we bring what is present, but absent, into view. Since everything is always in some degree absent or remote, understanding is necessary for perceptual consciousness.

Aesthetic Problems in Philosophy[8]

At the outset of this chapter (in the subsection entitled "Transformations of the Understanding") I called attention to the way in which aesthetic experience—the experience of the work of art—is an achievement of the understanding. The bare perceptual exposure to the song, or to the painting there on the wall in the gallery, is not yet the aesthetic experience. Aesthetic experience is achieved by interrogating what is there before you. To bring the work into focus, we need to acquire the skills needed to do this. And this we do on the fly, *in situ*, with the resources the world (the art work) provides. Through looking, handling, describing, conversing, noticing, comparing, keeping track, we achieve contact with the work/world. We achieve an appreciation of the way the piece hangs together—what the work is—through activities I will refer to collectively as aesthetic discourse, or better, criticism. We achieve the sort of understanding that consists in seeing connections, what Wittgenstein characterized as a perspicuous overview of the whole (1953, §122).

We learn our way around in a space of possibilities that the piece opens up.

Aesthetic criticism is thus a necessary accompaniment of the kind of perceptual achievement in which aesthetic experience consists. Criticism is the way we make the adjustments needed to make sense of

---

8. My subtitle here is meant to call to mind Stanley Cavell's wonderful essay "On Aesthetic Problems of Modern Philosophy."

what is before us. Aesthetic experience happens against the background of criticism.[9] This was Kant's conception. Aesthetic experience—for example, the sort of experience he characterized as that of the beautiful—has intersubjectively valid content. Our aesthetic experience of the work of art reflects our sense of what the work demands, not only of us, but of anyone. Our response thus reflects our sense of how one ought to respond to the work. Aesthetic experience happens only where there is the possibility of substantive disagreement, and so also the need for justification, explanation and persuasion. The work of art is only experienced when it is experienced as making claims on us, claims we need to adjudicate.

Kant was also clear that despite the fact that aesthetic experience is a thoughtful recognition of what the work demands—we must regard the experience as a cognitive achievement—it is nevertheless the case that aesthetic response is always also and fundamentally a matter of feeling, of responsiveness, rather than a matter of judgment. We don't engage in explicit deliberative reasoning to decide whether something is beautiful. There is literally no possibility of such reasoning. We can't convince ourselves or others of the beauty of a work. Rules, algorithms, criteria, have no place here.

And yet—crucially—we can try. We have to try, if we are to take our own aesthetic responses (our own aesthetic *judgments*) seriously. What we need to see is that there is a deployment of our cognitive faculties that is at once rigorous, and rational, but that does not require that it eventuate in a Q.E.D. We aim at persuasion, at clarification, at motivation, and indeed justification. I can't prove to you that something is beautiful, but I can teach you to see its beauty, and I can fault you for being unable or unwilling to do so.

Whether or not this is exactly Kant's view, it seems that Kant, like Wittgenstein, offers a picture of the way the intellect enlivens aesthetic experience which shows us how, to use John McDowell's Sellarsian phrasing, aesthetic experience is in the space of reason, even though, at one and the same time, there is no sense in which it is attached to explicit deliberative judgment. Crucially, as I would put it, the critical in-

---

9. This point is important. The existence of critical conversation about art is not a mere accidental by-product of art practices themselves, but an essential constituent of those practices.

quiry that the art work occasions and requires is the very means by which we exercise the understanding that brings the work of art into focus and so allows us to feel it, to be sensitive to it.

The pleasure of aesthetic experience, in my approach, is the pleasure of "getting it." It is the pleasure of understanding, of seeing connections, of comfortably knowing one's way about. It is the pleasure that comes from recognizing the purposiveness (*Zweckmässigkeit*, as Kant would have it), or integrity (as Dewey put it), or meaning, of the work. This meaning or purposiveness was there all along, but hidden in plain sight.

And so there can be no charge here of over-intellectualizing. What we need to admit, finally, is that there is a nonjudgmental use of concepts; a deployment of concepts in, as I put it earlier, a perceptual or experiential mode. We can say more about this here. Building on the idea, taken up also in Chapter 2, that understanding is akin to an ability, I propose that we think of concepts as tools for picking up features of the world around us, or techniques for grasping things, features, aspects, qualities. To learn a concept is to learn to grasp something (it is to acquire a *Begriff*; it is to learn to handle something, *etwas befgreifen*). What criticism affords is the cultivation of the understanding, the development and so the procurement of the conceptual tools that enable us to pick up what is there before us. Concepts are ways of achieving access to the world around us.

Art Is Philosophy

Art and philosophy are one; this is our surprising upshot. Philosophy aims at the kind of understanding that lets us find our way about and make contact with the world. Philosophy aims at the sort of understanding that an art work occasions and that aesthetic criticism produces. Philosophical discussion and argument is a modality of aesthetic discourse; it is a species of criticism. Philosophical arguments, no less than aesthetic ones, never end with a Q.E.D., pretensions of philosophers to the contrary notwithstanding. This troubled Plato in the *Meno* and it has continued to puzzle philosophy all along. Philosophy—and again, the same is true of art—is always troubled by itself, always seeking better to understand its project. We can see our way clear of this by recognizing that the value of philosophical conversation, like aesthetic conversation about a work of art, consists not in arrival at a settled conclusion, but rather in the achievement of the sort of understanding that enables one to bring the world, or the art work, or one's puzzles, into focus. This is the transformation we seek, in philosophy and in art.

We also see that the conception of aesthetic experience I am articulating here—incorporating as it does elements from Kant and Wittgenstein—is really a conception of perceptual experience *tout court*. All perceptual experience is a matter of bringing the world into focus by achieving the right kind of skillful access to it, the right kind of understanding. Art matters because art recapitulates this basic fact about perceptual consciousness. Art is human experience, in the small, and so it is, in a way, a model or guide to our basic situation. Art is philosophy. And all perceptual experience, viewed correctly, is a kind of aesthetic experience.

And so, the encounter with the world, like the encounter with a work of art, unfolds against the background of aesthetic conversation. Perception is not a matter of sensation; it is never a matter of mere feeling. Perceiving is an activity of securing access to the world by cultivating the right critical stance, that is, by cultivating the right understanding.

It is easy to lose track of the thoughtful and rhetorical structure of human experience. For example, it is sometimes noticed that contents of experience do not enter into logical relations with other contentful states. Perception does not entail belief; and belief does not rule out countervailing perceptual experience. This is sometimes taken to show that experience and belief have different kinds of content, that the content of the former cannot be conceptual in the way that the latter is. Examples like the Müller-Lyer illusion have been adduced to demonstrate this.[10] The fact that the lines can look different in length even when I know they are the same is thought to show that the content of the perceptual experience cannot be logically structured in the way that the corresponding belief is structured.

But this is a gross mistake. Nothing requires us to say that concepts are brought into play in the one case, but not the other; all that we are compelled to say, rather, is that there are different ways for them to be brought into play. To suppose that the contents are truly incommensurable, rather than that they are in conflict, say, is not to offer an expla-

---

10. See, for example, Gareth Evans's *Varieties of Reference* (1982).

nation of the phenomenon of conflict between what we see and what we know. It is to explain it away, or really, to deny the phenomenon itself.

The big mistake is the overlooking of the aesthetic, or critical, character and context of all experience. There is *no such thing* as how things look independently of this larger context of thought, feeling and interest. What we know and what we see push and pull against each other, and they move each other and guide each other and tutor each other. This is plain and obvious when we think of the experience of art. It is no less true in daily life. What makes it almost impossible to appreciate this in the present case—the Müller-Lyer illusion—is the cartoonish simplicity of the case. The rhetorical context is so impoverished that it seems, mistakenly, as if context is irrelevant, and so, as if we have uncovered something deep and primitive in the workings of the visual system, namely, its cognitive impenetrability. But really, the psychologist has pulled a fast one on us.

The Puzzles of Phenomenology

An important upshot of taking aesthetic experience to be the very paradigm of a perceptual experience is that it lets us see our way clear to a better conception of the nature of phenomenology.

Consider three puzzles about phenomenology as traditionally or conventionally construed.

First, a long-standing worry is that introspection is fuzzy. Traditional approaches take for granted that experience is a matter of introspection, for they take for granted that the experience is something that happens inside you that supports and accompanies your action. But introspection is a we-know-not-what. What are we supposed to be looking for? And how do we know when we've found it? How can we be sure we are describing it accurately? These unanswered questions befuddle any attempt to take introspection seriously as a method. Once we give up the idea that experiences are internal events, we can more or less leave introspection aside.

Second, there is a well-known worry about transparency.[11] When we turn our attention to our experiences of seeing, hearing, touching,

---

11. E.g. G. E. Moore, Gilbert Ryle.

we almost inevitably turn our attention to what we see, or hear, or touch. It seems that the experience is invisible to us, for it is transparent and we find ourselves seeing right through it to the other side, to the world itself. A similar problem arises when we try to think about the visual field. If we turn our attention to the visual field, we almost inevitably end up turning our attention to that which is before us, to the world. Several philosophers have noticed this and have grappled with the question: given the transparency of experience, such as it is, how can it ever be possible to investigate the character of experience itself?

Third, Dreyfus, Sean Kelly, Sartre, and others, have emphasized a certain phenomenological paradox, to wit, that when we turn our attention to our experience, we actually modify the character of our experience. In the free flow of experience, there is only, for example, the bus I am trying to catch, or the painting on the wall I want to see. We naturally and spontaneously respond to the world and we do so in a way that shows we are sensitive to the world's solicitations. We step back to achieve the point of optimum grip on the picture; we lunge around the passers-by in our effort to capture the bus driver's attention. But nowhere does the experience itself, as an episode in consciousness, show up for me. Indeed, I am myself absent from the story. And when we stop and contrive to think about what we saw and felt and "experienced," well, then we are in a completely different, reflective, contemplative, detached domain. No matter how sensitively I try to make explicit why or how I adjusted myself to get a better view of the picture on the wall, I cannot make explicit that which was implicitly operative in my consciousness. For even it is of the essence of the phenomenon we seek to describe that nothing was in that way explicit in it.

We can begin to see our way clear to a new way of responding to these puzzles. Phenomenology does not require that we turn our attention away from the world, that we introspect, or that we try to defeat experience's transparency. Phenomenology requires, rather, that we turn our attention to what we are doing, to our engaged activity. And we actually have a paradigm of what it would be to do this: aesthetic criticism.

Experience is not something that happens in us. It is something we do. Experience itself as a kind of dance—a dynamic of involvement and engagement with the world around us. To study the experience, we must study the dance. The aesthetic task of bringing a dance itself into focus for perceptual consciousness—the task we undertake when we grapple with live performance, for example, whether as a member of the audience, or as a performer—is exactly the same as that which we confront when we wish to undertake an investigation of our own experience. Aesthetic criticism can be our model.

The phenomenological stance, then, is the aesthetic stance, and the aesthetic stance is available to us both as performers (or agents) or as critics (or members of the audience). Dreyfus and Sartre are right that I can't contemplate my experience of running for the bus, as I run for the bus. But there is no call for this sort of self-monitoring (neither on the part of the performer or the critic). Paying attention to yourself, or to what is going on inside you, is one thing, and paying attention to the task at hand, to what you are doing, is another. And *that* is what is required of the aesthetic stance: a critical awareness of and sensitivity to what you are doing.

Bringing Ourselves into Focus

To summarize what we have accomplished so far: experience is active and it is thoughtful; it is intellectual, but it also sensual; it is rule-governed, and the question of which rules govern us, why and how, always arises. But that does not mean that we must in fact always be able to give a certain answer or that we can make it all explicit.

I want now to address a worry that stems from a problem about animal minds. If experience is always aesthetic, if it always takes place in a setting where criticism and philosophy are also in place, then can there be any sense at all to the idea that nonhuman animals have experience? What is aesthetic criticism in the life of the dog? Or the whale? This question has a certain urgency for me, since, after all, part of what has motivated me to develop a practical, active, tool-like conception of concepts and the understanding (in Chapter 6 of *Action in Perception*) was precisely to open up the possibility of appreciating the continuity between animal and human minds. By locating experience in the setting of a narrative drama of a striving to achieve skill-based access to the world, have I not simply reintroduced the necessity of there being a very sharp line between them and us all over again?

The problem of consciousness, as I understand it now, is that of understanding how the world shows up for us. The problem of consciousness is the problem of the world's presence to mind. How the world shows up for us depends not only on our brains and nervous systems, but also on our bodies, our skills, our environment, the way we are placed in and at home in the world. The world shows up for us thanks to what we can do—to the way we can achieve access—and this depends not only on us (on our brains and bodily makeup), but also on the world around us and our relation to it. We make complicated adjustments to bring the world into focus.

This is so for animals as well as humans. We move and peer and squint and reach and handle and respond and so we skillfully take hold of what there is around us. We achieve access to the world. We enact it by enabling it to show up for us. Sometimes we fail. There are different ways we can fail to achieve access to the world; there are different ways the world can fail to show up for us. If the skills needed to pick up a feature are absent, then the feature is not present in our experience. If I don't have the relevant skills of literacy, for example, the words written on the wall do not show up for me. I can't see them, even though they are there. I lack the skills. This is just the way the words can fail to show up for infant children, or for my dog.

But there is a way we adult humans can get lost, or confused, a way we can fail to secure the world, which is not available to children or animals. We can find the very techniques, technologies, skills and practices that open up the world for us in the first place to be the source of puzzlement. As Heidegger put it, we can be a problem to ourselves.

Adult human persons are smarter than animals and children. At least some of them are. We are smart enough to be not only skillful, but ironic. We are smart enough to be confused by the complicated choreographies of our own transactions with the world around us. And so we are driven to philosophy and art. For philosophy and art—we have seen, these are really one—are our main way of grappling with the anxiety caused by our predicament.

Animal and infant experience is no less complicated; it is no less enacted than our own. It's just that animals, children, and perhaps some grown-up humans, are not able to perceive the puzzling character of our own being. They aren't anxious. They aren't a problem to themselves.

I readily admit that what I have said here is simply to redescribe what we already know: that human adults have intellectual and mental lives unlike those of animals and children. What I try to secure, through this redescription, is an appreciation of the fact that perceptual consciousness—experience—is what we share with other living creatures, and not something we possess apart. It is precisely the aesthetic character of experience—that it is performed in dynamic exchange with the world around us—that brings this fact about our mutual nature into focus.

7

※

Ideology and the Third Realm

Or, a Short Essay on Knowing How to Philosophize

"Es geht nicht darum, Philosophie zu kennen;
sondern philosophieren zu können."

—Martin Heidegger

"No philosophic argument ends with Q.E.D.
However forceful, it never forces. There is
no bullying in philosophy, neither with the
stick of logic nor with the stick of language."

—Friedrich Waismann

The Problem of the Third Realm

FREGE claimed that statements of number are statements about concepts (1884/1978, 59). The statement "the King's carriage is drawn by four horses," for example, is a statement about the concept "horse that draws the King's carriage." It might look as if we are talking about the King's carriage, when we use these words, but we aren't. What we are saying, according to Frege, is that the concept "horse that draws the King's carriage" is true of exactly four things.

This is not the only case Frege brings to our attention where, in a sense, we fail to understand what we are saying. Here is another example: we aren't talking about whales when we say that whales are mammals; our topic, rather, is the relation between the two concepts "whale" and "mammal," viz. that anything that falls under the first also falls under the second (Frege 1884/1978, 60).

Let's say Frege is right: appearances notwithstanding, a statement of number is a statement about a concept; or: we're talking about concepts, not whales, when we say whales are mammals. The questions I pose are these: What sort of discovery is this? How does Frege know? If he were mistaken, what would he be mistaken about? And what kind of mistake is it that we are guilty of when we naïvely find ourselves believing that we are talking about the King's carriage, or horses, when we say "the King's carriage is drawn by four horses"? Frege's accomplishment is impressive, especially when placed in coordination with his analysis of existence and quantification. But what is his accomplishment exactly?

A reflection on Frege's practice suggests two interesting and puzzling features of his analysis.

First, the proposal that a statement of number is a statement about a concept does not seem to be the sort of thesis that admits of definitive proof. We don't have any idea what such a proof would look like. Frege can give us reasons for agreeing with him, and he does, but he can't quite compel our assent. There isn't anything like a Q.E.D. in the offing here. We can speak of getting what he's trying to show; we can speak of getting it right; we can speak of being persuaded. But there are no decision procedures here that would enable us to decide, as it were once and for all, that in fact we're talking about concepts and not whales or numbers.

If this is right—and this is hardly shocking—then *analysis,* in the relevant sense, isn't like chemical analysis. In chemistry we have microscopes that allow us to peer into the internal structure of materials and we have solvents and other chemicals that allow us to break a compound into its component parts. But in the domain of philosophical analysis that is our concern, there isn't anything that plays the role of solvent, or microscope. There are no independent or objective measures in this domain.[1]

Second, for all that there are no rules or decision procedures for evaluating claims about what we really mean when we say that that the King's carriage is drawn by four horses, it would be crazy to think that Frege isn't offering us a substantive thesis, a thesis that is either right or wrong. We may not know how to settle the matter once and for all, but we can't doubt that we are in a realm of intersubjectively significant discussion; we encounter here the live possibility of agreement and

---

1. I do not mean to be taking a stand on the question of whether we ought to be realists about sciences like chemistry. There are those who would hold that chemical realities are only available to us against the background of the grid-work of our methodologies, technologies, methods of representation, and the like. Whatever we say about that, this has no bearing on my claim here that in chemistry, and in other sciences, we enjoy a clear sense of what our objectives are and a clear sense of how to decide whether we have achieved them. Chemistry is entirely sharable and intersubjective. My point in this chapter is that philosophy does not seem to be like this, even though it does not seem to be subjective either.

disagreement. Indeed, Frege offers reasons for his proposal; he makes an argument that goes something like this: If we aren't talking about the concept "horse that draws the King's carriage," then, he asks us, what are we talking about? The King's carriage? But there is only *one* of those. The horses? Are we saying that the horses are four? Is this like saying that they are brown? If it is, then it ought to follow that each of them is four, just as it would follow that each of them is brown. But *that* isn't what we want to say. Is four then supposed to be a property not of the horses individually but of the collective? At best it is arbitrary to assign the number four to the collective. We might just as well assign the number one because there is one collective, or the number two because there are two pair of horses. No, Frege says, we aren't talking about *things* at all, and we aren't ascribing properties to things. Number words are not adjectives. A statement of number is not about a thing; it is, rather, a statement about a way we have of thinking about a thing, which is to say, it is a statement about a concept.

Are you persuaded? I am. But that is of no matter. What is important is that we appreciate that Frege is trying to persuade us of something. He is offering an analysis of what we mean when we engage in a certain type of thought and talk about number. And either he gets it right, or he doesn't.

If we wish to understand philosophical analysis—this is the topic—then we need to understand the distinctively in-between—neither entirely objective nor merely subjective—character of claims about, for example, what we really mean or what we are really talking about. We need to make sense of the fact that analytical insight into the character of our thought and talk, whether Frege's or Socrates's, takes place neither in a realm like chemistry, which is, so to speak, straightforwardly objective, nor in a realm that is merely subjective, where there is no call for reason-giving and argument. Frege's insights into our thought and talk belong in neither of these realms, but rather in a *third* realm. To understand philosophical analysis, we need to understand the character of this third realm. This is our challenge.

An Inadequate Experimentalism

I can imagine that there are philosophers—let's call them experimental philosophers—who think Frege should have taken a vote.

Their policy would be to send out a questionnaire with a multiple-choice question along these lines:

The sentence "The King's carriage is drawn by four horses" is a statement about which of the following:
  (a) the King's carriage,
  (b) the horses,
  (c) the concept "horse that draws the King's carriage,"
  (d) none of the above.

Once we recognize the third-realm character of Frege's problems, and ours, the misguidedness of this experimentalist approach becomes immediately apparent. The point is not that Frege or we are entitled to be indifferent to what people say or would say in answer to such a questionnaire. The point is that whatever people say could be at most the beginning of our conversation, not its end; it would be the opportunity for philosophy, not the determination of the solution of a philosophical problem.

The experimentalist displays a naïveté that amounts to a blindness to philosophy and its challenges. The experimentalist's approach is tantamount to a denial of the third-realm character of the analysis problem. Such a statistical procedure could only be justified, after all, if we think that there is a straightforward decision procedure for deciding what people think (e.g. taking a headcount), or, barring that, if we think that there is no fact of the matter at all about what people really mean and that the best we can do is gather data about what people say they mean. But the question—what do people really think about this or that?, like the question, what do they really like?—are third-realm questions: there is no decision procedure (empirical or otherwise) for answering them, but this is not to say that they are empty questions.

The experimentalist may be motivated by a desire to repudiate dogmatism. When backed into a corner by hostile Indians, the Lone Ranger is said to have turned to Tonto and exclaimed: "What are we to do?" Tonto's reply: "Who do you mean by 'we,' white man?"[2] And so we can appreciate that there is something potentially misguided about thinking that *we* can decide, from the armchair, what people really mean. If

---

2. Daniel Dennett told me this joke in 1995. I have the impression that it is widely known.

we are interested in what people really mean, then we'd better interrogate people themselves.

A fair point. But what is needed, then, is an interrogation, or better, a conversation or dialogue, with the people whose thinking we wish better to understand. The Lone Ranger joke in a way perpetuates a misunderstanding. After all, the Lone Ranger's reply to Tonto ought to have been clear. "Who do I mean by 'we'? I mean, you, Tonto, and me. We're in this predicament together." Whose laughter matters when you tell a joke? The people to whom you tell the joke. And so in the philosophical case. To return to Frege's case: it is *we* who are puzzled by our use of number words, once we've read Frege at least. It seems as if we use number words as adjectives, to ascribe properties to things. But this can't be right. Consider my deck of cards. It is *one* deck. But it is fifty-two cards. And who knows how many atoms. What number attaches to the deck of cards *really?* The problem is our problem. And we aren't interested in data points about what people say. Just as it doesn't help me understand whether I value a book I have read to learn that it is on the best-seller list. And it is of no use to be told *why* it is on the best-seller list. The question I must care about is something more like: does it deserve to be? We are interested in the question of what we ourselves mean, in why we say what we say, or in why we feel we can't say anything else. It is our puzzlement, our sense of surprise, or revelation, that is our subject matter. If you say, "It's one thing, the deck," I'll say, "Yes, but then don't you mean that there is here before us *one* instance of the concept 'is a deck of cards'?" I might add: "You don't means that the deck is one, the way the deck is new, do you?" And so we go on, and on. Until we come to a point where we can stop. Or until we lose patience with each other. Or until we recognize that there isn't a way to settle the issue between us.

To deny the third-realm character of our puzzle, as the experimentalist does, is to lapse, however unintentionally, into a distinct species of dogmatism. And it is to miss the point of, and the opportunity for, philosophy.

It is perhaps useful to state clearly that to reject the inadequate experimentalism, and to insist on the third-realm character of philosophical problems, is neither to set philosophy over against the natural sciences, nor is it to deny that mind and experience can be made the subject of natural scientific investigation. To reject the inadequate experimentalism is not to reject naturalism in this sense.

It is, however, to acknowledge that the demands of naturalism are not always clear, and, indeed, they are sometimes unclear precisely because the study of nature is not itself neatly segregated from the problems of philosophy.

The thing that needs to be emphasized is that philosophical problems are not the property of philosophy professors. Philosophy arises for natural science; it arises within natural science. To insist on the impossibility of reducing philosophy to natural science is to acknowledge that natural science is also and must remain, at least sometimes, a philosophical practice. Philosophy does not stand opposed to natural science. Philosophy is one of science's moments; or maybe, natural science is one of philosophy's moments. A naturalized philosophy will not seek to replace philosophical conversation with experiments. It will acknowledge the unbreakable marriage of philosophy and natural science.

A Misguided Antipsychologism

Frege's insight into the character of our thought and talk was profound. But it turns out that he himself was no better able than the experimentalist to appreciate the third-realm character of his achievements. Frege fails to offer a satisfying account of the status of his own insight.

Frege is sometimes credited with showing that grammatical form is a poor guide to the underlying logical form of our thoughts (see, for example, Anscombe 1959). The problem with this characterization is that it suggests that Frege's conception of the relation between thought and language is coherent, when in fact it would seem to have been anything but. On the one hand, Frege insists that thought is not in any way essentially tied to language. There could be beings who were able to grasp thoughts directly, without needing to clad them in the sensible garb of language (Frege 1924, 288). On the other hand, Frege insists that we are not such creatures. For human beings, at least, the grasping of thoughts is tied to linguistic understanding.[3] More importantly, his declarations to the contrary notwithstanding, Frege conceives of thoughts as quasi-linguistic entities. The thought, after all, is the sense of a sen-

---

3. Frege writes: "There is no contradiction in supposing there to exist beings that can grasp the same thought as we do without needing to clad it in a form that can be perceived by the senses. But still, for us men there is this necessity" (1924, 288).

tence (Frege 1918–1919, 61), and to the constituents of the thought there correspond constituents of the sentence (at least a sentence in the language of pure thought, what Frege called the concept-script). A thought, for Frege, then, is the kind of thing whose essence can be exhibited in a suitably clarified formal symbolism.

Part of what prevents Frege from providing an adequate conception of his own analytical insights is his celebrated and, for all that, misguided antipsychologism. Logic has nothing to do with psychology, argued Frege. The logician isn't interested in how we think, but in how we ought to think (1918–1919 pp. 58, 59). Psychology is concerned with ideas, which, for Frege, as for Locke or Hume, are purely interior occurrences, rather like tickles or sensations. On Frege's understanding of what an idea is, I have my ideas, and you have yours, and there is no sense whatsoever to the possibility that we might speak about them, compare them, share them. Ideas are private (Frege 1918–1919, 67). In contrast with ideas, which arise in my head and yours, but can never pass forth between us, thoughts can be communicated. They may be immaterial, like ideas, but unlike ideas, they can be shared and grasped and communicated. Thoughts are not private. Their immateriality is no obstacle to their mind-independence and their actuality.

A thought, for Frege, is real and self-standing, like a walnut or a pistol. And like walnuts and pistols, thoughts can be *grasped*. But unlike walnuts and pistols, thoughts are *immaterial;* they exist outside of space in time in what Frege himself called a third realm. And so we can reasonably ask: How do we grasp thoughts? How do we come into contact with them? Frege's attitude to these questions was ambivalent. On the one hand, he insists that these questions are of no relevance to logic; they are the province of psychology. On the other hand, Frege seems to have appreciated that, at least as he sets up the problems, these are questions that can't be answered. Remember, Frege allows the possibility that there might be creatures capable of a direct apprehension of thoughts, without any linguistic or communicative setting. Thoughts, and the place they occupy in our lives, for Frege, are a mystery.[4]

---

4. "When a thought is grasped, it at first only brings about changes in the inner world of the one who grasps it; yet it remains untouched in the core of its essence, for the changes it undergoes affect only inessential properties. There is lacking here something we observe everywhere in physical process—reciprocal action. Thoughts are not wholly unac-

The irony is this: Frege's strange melding of a radically subjectivist view of psychology with a realist/objectivist view of thoughts makes it entirely obscure how Frege's own insight into the structure of our sayings could even be possible. Frege's ontology renders his own analytic practice incomprehensible. For what was Frege's investigation other than an investigation into how we understand our thought and talk (about numbers, concepts, etc.). By insisting that grasping a thought is coming into contact with something whose fundamental nature is independent of our thinking, talking and understanding (for these are the province of psychology), Frege does not merely render thoughts occult; he renders the very possibility of comprehending the real, transcendent structure of thoughts an enigma, and precisely because their nature is now thought of as transcendent. Philosophical analysis, in this view, *is* like chemistry; but it is a mysterious chemistry that requires of us that we achieve bald insight into the mind-independent reality of substances.

The Structure of Our Practices

I have been speaking of Frege's insight, and now also of Frege's mistake. His mistake prevents him from understanding the nature of his own insight. His mistake consists in a failure to bring the third-realm character of his own investigations into focus.

In an effort to bring light to the issue, let us, for a moment, consider baseball. Baseball is not merely a system of rules and representations. To learn baseball is not merely to learn rules that define a class of events as baseball events (base hits, runs, foul balls, etc.) and that define others as *non*baseball events (foot faults, touchdowns, for example). To learn the game is to learn, among other things, to *perceive* these events, to notice, for example, a missed scoring opportunity, or a nicely turned double play. It is also to learn to take an interest in occurrences such as these. The baseball aficionado *cares* whether the pickoff attempt was

---

tual but their actuality is quite different from the actuality of things. And their action is brought about by a performance of the thinker; without this they would be inactive, at least as far as we can see. And yet the thinker does not create them but must take them as they are. They can be true without being grasped by a thinker; and they are not wholly unactual even then, at least if they could be grasped and so brought into action" (Frege 1918–1919, 77).

botched; he or she is emotionally involved in the course of play. To learn baseball is to learn to be engaged with baseball; it is to enter into what we might call *the baseball world*.

There is more to say about this initiation into the baseball world. A striking feature of life in the baseball world is the importance, indeed the urgency, attached to talk and thought about baseball, about its play, its history, and also its problems. It belongs to life in the baseball world that we engage in elaborate critical discourse *about* baseball. This critical discourse is about baseball, but it is also, I would suggest, *constitutive of* baseball. In baseball we not only hit, field, throw and run, we also dispute calls at the plate, we question the application of the rules, and take sides on hard cases, and we even worry about whether rulebook reforms are necessary to avoid certain situations in the future. A crucial feature of the baseball world—and here it is comparable to the legal world, for example,—is that the first-order practice contains and requires its own metatheory (as I discussed in the introduction and Chapter 2). Or to put the point a different way: baseball requires and nurtures its own ideology.

Are there really home runs and strikeouts, infield pop-ups and outs at home plate? Do these things exist? Of course they do. That the fly ball cleared the wall in fair territory is an intersubjectively assessable matter of fact. Whether it happened is one thing, whether you or I or anyone believe it happened is another.[5] To doubt the real, mind-independent existence of home runs would be like doubting the reality of taxes, say, or race.

Of course there are those who insist, quite reasonably, on the unreality of race (for example) on the grounds that we lack (I assume this for the sake of argument) any social practice-independent account of what race is; for example, we lack a plausible biological theory of race. It would be a mistake, though, to think that this fact—that race is not biological—

---

5. Actually, this is a complicated issue, precisely because of the curious status in baseball of the umpire. An umpire calls plays; intuitively, he can get the calls right or wrong. Certainly, baseball audiences frequently criticize umpires for "blown" calls. But this misunderstands the role of the umpire. He is not an outsider; in a sense he is not a judge at all. The umpire is not a person with opinions, but is rather a mechanism of baseball play. And as a matter of fact, except in exceptional circumstances, an umpire's actions cannot be overturned. An umpire's call makes it the case that a player is safe or out; it does not record this fact.

means that there is no race. After all, there is good evidence to the contrary. Race is a statistically significant factor determining measurable features of the lives of real people (such as, e.g. income, life expectancy, etc.). Race is something of which we find ourselves drawn to say both that it exists and that it does not exist. "Race is nothing, a figment!" "Race is a defining feature of our lives in modern society!" To understand race, we need to take the measure of this somewhat paradoxical situation.

I think we would all agree that it would be lunacy to reply to the antirealist about home runs or race by insisting that home runs and race are abstract, Platonic phenomena residing outside space and time. What makes this lunatic is that our best hope of understanding what a home run is would be to think about the place of home runs in an actual baseball-playing practice. A home run is not something that exists outside of baseball, anymore than a checkmate is something that exists within baseball. To try to understand the existence of home runs as entities that are autonomous of baseball practice would be to pull the rug out from under one's only hope of understanding what a home run is. And something very much like this needs to be said about race. Race can only be understood in the context of a set of historical circumstances and conditions, conditions that include among themselves facts concerning social attitudes about, precisely, race. Race is something we make in our social practice. We enact race. We do so in millions of ways (some beautiful and some not).

I would like to suggest that Frege's attitudes about language and thought are comparable to the admittedly lunatic view about baseball. The corresponding lunacy, however, is much harder to appreciate when we turn to language. We take our own ideologies about language so much for granted, that we find it literally ridiculous to try to see things from a different point of view. Our entrenchment in the language world is so profound that we find it difficult to appreciate the practice relativity of our linguistic ontologies. Are there nouns and verbs, sentences and truth values, concepts and concept-expressions? This question is like the question about fly balls and double plays. Of course there are! It is however to misunderstand these questions completely to suppose that linguistic entities have any reality outside the corresponding social practices. But crucially, this is exactly what Frege does when he supposes that a concept, for example, is an abstract constituent of thoughts. (And this is exactly what linguists do when they suppose that language is fixed in the human genome, that it is an element of our biological endowment.[6])

The basic point here is that our judgments about concepts and meaning, as about grammaticality and words, are judgments we make *within* the language world, just as reflections on baseball are made within the baseball world. Frege's indifference to this point—and as far as I can tell, the indifference of most practitioners of philosophy of language, as well as "scientific" linguistics—forces him to conceive of language and thought in ways that divorce it from our lives, from our practices, from our actions.

I am not the first to compare language to games. Nevertheless, there is still a great deal to be learned from the comparison. Here is something else. Notice that a home run isn't merely something it is possible to do in baseball. A home run is a thing of a very definite value. If you are batting, a home run is *very* good. If you are pitching, a home run is *very* bad. To understand what a home run is to understand, *inter alia*, that every batter wants to hit one and every pitcher wants to do whatever is possible to avoid giving one up. In general, it isn't possible to separate moves in games from their value, from their point. Exactly the same thing can and ought to be said about linguistic moves. Speech happens in the setting of our active lives. To make a statement is to achieve something, and very often it is also to achieve something else—you inform someone of something, you frighten, threaten or amuse another, you close a deal or break off relations or invite some further exchange. To understand language is to understand the ways in which language is deployed in the different settings of our active lives.

To learn a language is not only to learn to use words, it is to learn to think about, criticize and reflect on the use of words. This is a striking feature of all linguistic communities and is clearly in evidence when

---

6. This is a complicated topic and one that I can't do justice here. But notice, to the linguist's reply that language is universal, one might reasonably respond, no it isn't! English and Hausa are about as universal as baseball is. To which the linguist is likely to retort: granted, individual languages are not universal, but *Language* is. And the evidence for this? At this point the linguist will point to deep structures and principles that are true of all languages. My response, to be filled out elsewhere: these judgments are made within the language-world, just as baseball judgments are made in the baseball world. They have no practice-independent plausibility. One example: the linguist helps him or herself to the idea of a "sentence," an idea that is on a par, ontologically, with that of "home run."

adults talk to children. We don't merely teach kids how to talk, we teach them the concepts "how you say ___" and "what ___ means," and we teach them to criticize the use of words with expressions such as: "no, not like *that*, like *this*." To learn a language is to learn a theory of language, just as to learn baseball is to learn a theory of baseball. Language, like baseball, comes packaged with ideology. There are no ideologically neutral linguistic judgments.

A Concept Is Akin to an Ability

We have noticed that Frege's mystical ontology of thought and language blinded him to the status of his own insights about structure and meaning. It also sometimes led him to astonishing and perverse claims. The idea that sentences stand for the True or the False, the way names stand for their bearers, is one such example (Frege 1891, 15; 1892, 34). A perhaps more egregious example is Frege's insistence that concepts must be sharply delimited, that is, defined for every object thought of as argument (Frege 1891, 20).[7] A concept such as that of "is greater than"—as when we say that 3 is greater than 2—is not well-defined, according to Frege, if it is not determinate whether, say, the moon is greater than Julius Caesar. And likewise, we haven't succeeded in explaining what a given number is—the number 1 say—if we can't explain not only why (for example) 1 is the result of subtracting 2 from 3, but also, why 1 is not identical to Julius Caesar.

What is striking, in this demand of Frege's, is the extent to which Frege has severed the link between concepts and our understanding and practice. It would be crazy to tell a child he'd failed to grasp addition because he could make neither heads nor tails of the addition of Julius Caesar and the moon.[8] This would be like criticizing a child for

---

7. "This involves the requirement, as regards concepts, that, for any argument, they shall have a truth-value as their value; that it shall be determinate, for any object, whether it falls under the concept or not. In other words: as regards concepts we have a requirement of sharp delimitation . . ." (Frege 1891, 20). Frege explains that we must be able to say what the sum of the sun + 1 is, if our concept of addition is to be of any use at all. If we can't answer the question of the sum of the sun and 1, then we can't with any confidence speak of the sum of 10 and 1 either.

8. In *The Foundations of Arithmetic* (1884/1978), Frege insists it is a scandalous that no mathematician can state what the number 1 is. Of course, this is not a scandal; inability to say what 1 is does not count (not in Frege's day, not now) as evidence that one is deficient

being unable to score a touchdown in baseball. There's no move here, no space in the practice. Concepts are *not* defined over all possible objects; our use of concepts has a point and occurs in a context (just as with strikes and home runs). To miss this is to think of understanding as a matter of the manipulation of formal symbols. But that's to leave understanding out of the story.

A concept is literally a technique for grasping hold of something in thought (as the etymology of the word reveals, and as I have discussed in previous chapters). Frege, like Kant before him, took for granted that concepts are predicates of judgment. But this is certainly mistaken if it therefore follows that the only use to which we can put a concept is in the making of a judgment. If I have the concept, home run, then I can judge of a fly ball that it is a home run. But my grasp of the concept also enables me to see home runs, to encounter them, to recognize them when they occur around me. And it is surely to *over-intellectualize* one's experience of the ball game to suppose that each case of concept-dependent recognition is an *act of judgment.* Indeed, it is precisely this sort of *intellectualist* error that is one of Frege's lasting legacies.

The Intellectualist Mistake

Frege's mistake—his inability to bring the third-realm character of philosophical discourse into focus—can be called the intellectualist mistake. For it forces Frege to conceive of language and concepts as divorced from practice. The puzzle about the strict delimitation of concepts is a clear example of this.

Frege failed to allow for the possibility of a perceptual, nonjudgmental use of concepts. This is a signal commitment of the intellectualist. It is worth noticing that this same mistake is made by many philosophers we might call anti-intellectualist. For example, some philosophers have insisted that to suppose that perception is in whole or in part conceptual runs the risk of over-intellectualizing perceptual experience, as if the only role for concepts is in the making of explicit delib-

---

in arithmetical knowledge. It is worth noticing, though, that Frege didn't merely insist on pressing the demand for an answer to the question, "What is the number 1?," he actually devised new conceptual/mathematical tools for framing an answer. After Frege it becomes possible at least to imagine what an answer to the question "What is the number 1?" might look like, even if Frege's own answer can no longer be taken seriously.

erative judgments (e.g. Hurley 2001; Dreyfus 2006). But this is precisely to over-intellectualize the intellect itself (exactly as Frege did). The use of concepts, like the use of tools, is a practical achievement. It is nonetheless an intellectual one for all that. Talking, playing chess, these are spheres of intellectual accomplishment *par excellence*. This is compatible with the thought that these are also spheres where we can act without self-monitoring or deliberation, where we can be in the flow.

Or consider those who object to the idea that experience can be conceptual on the grounds that we don't have concepts of everything we can see (e.g. Evans 1982). Such a view again thinks of concepts as like words in a dictionary. Of course we don't have, antecedently, words for everything. But that is not to say that we can't embrace what we see in thought (as McDowell 1994 has argued; see also Noë 2004, Chapter 6).

Empiricists (such as John Campbell 2002) hold that we need to be able to see without concepts, because seeing provides the basis for acquiring concepts. But to see something is anyway just a way of getting a grip on what is there. It is just a special way of thinking about what is there. It is a kind of thought.

Practical Knowledge

Intellectualism is alive and well. This is one of Frege's legacies. And indeed, it is alive and well in good measure because as a culture we have failed to take up the challenge of making sense of the third realm where philosophy happens. And so we continue to shoehorn our problems into one or the other realm, into the objective or the subjective.

An impressive example of this is Stanley and Williamson's (2001) article on practical knowledge. They declare that it "is *simply false* . . . that ascriptions of knowledge-how ascribe abilities" (416, my italics). This is like claiming that it is simply false that we are talking about whales when we say that they are mammals. *Simply false?* As if there were a straightforward, unproblematic standard to which one can appeal, to which one must accede. But the third-realm character of analysis problems consists precisely in the fact that no such standards can be taken for granted. Which is not to say that we cannot advocate on behalf of certain standards. But then we need to press forward and argue. We can't appeal to what is *simply* true or false.

Consider the considerations they offer in defense of their claim. They write:

> For example, a ski instructor may know how to perform a certain complex stunt, without being able to perform it herself. Similarly, a master pianist who loses both of her arms in a tragic car accident still knows how to play the piano. But she has lost her ability to do so. (Stanley and Williamson 2001, 416)

Good points. But they are not dispositive. They do not round off and close down debate; they merely initiate it. Consider that one might with justification respond: abilities have enabling conditions. The fact that there is no water around makes it the case that I cannot swim, even though the absence of water does not deprive me of my ability to swim. That is, the fact that I can't exercise my ability does not make it the case that I have lost the ability. So there are two different ways one can fail to be able to do something. This is relevant to the case of the pianist. In losing her arms, one might argue, she has not lost the ability to play; she just can't exercise the ability (because relevant enabling conditions are not met; she has no arms).

There are other strategies one might explore in an attempt to resist Stanley and Williamson's assertion. One might, for example, concede that loss of the arms is not like the absence of a piano; to lose one's arms is to lose one's ability (not merely an enabling condition of the exercise of the ability). At the same time one might insist that thus to lose one's ability is to lose one's know-how as well.[9]

---

9. Bengson, Moffett, and Wright (forthcoming) demonstrate that a significant sample of people find nothing at all strange in the thought that know-how and corresponding abilities come apart. They ask respondents whether an injured ski jumper still knows how to do a quintuple Salchow, even though, because of injury, she can't actually do the jump. They find that two-thirds of responds say yes, demonstrating that "knowing how to do something" does not entail "being able to do it." They suggest this undermines the claims of Noë (2005) to the effect that in normal practice ascriptions of know-how entail ascriptions of corresponding abilities. Bengson, Moffett, and Wright's treatment of these issues is always careful and certainly fair. But I remain unpersuaded by their analysis. First, as I have remarked, "knowing how to do something" is systematically ambiguous as between "knowing how something is done" and "being able to do it" (Noë 2005, 275). And of course there is no incompatibility between knowing how something is done and being unable to do it. The relevance of this observation has recently been confirmed empirically by Jon Ellis in a not yet published paper. When Ellis first asked subjects whether the jumper still knew how one performs the jump, and only then asked whether

Whether you find this line of reasoning persuasive, what is clear is that it is pointless to suggest that it is *simply false* to think that ascriptions of know-how ascribe abilities. It is of the nature of the case that it is possible reasonably to explain away anything Stanley and Williamson might say to the contrary. Ditto for the case of the ski instructor. Nothing about the way the case is described entails that the ski instructor knows how to perform the stunt. What she knows is how the stunt is done, but to know how something is done is not (necessarily) to know how to do it.

Like Frege, and the experimentalists, Stanley and Williamson seem to think there is a big stick they can use to decide hard cases. And the big stick they have in mind is "recent syntactic theory." So much for the worst for this branch of linguistics.

Part of what makes the case of Stanley and Williamson particularly interesting is that it is their aim not merely to establish the point that there is no special linkage between practical knowledge and the possession of corresponding abilities, they wish to show that there is no *fundamental* distinction between practical and propositional knowledge. And they're right about this, as our reflection on the baseball case allows us to appreciate. If you know how to play baseball, then you can run, throw, field and catch, but you also know *that* each side has no more than nine players in the game at once, and *that* three strikes make an out. Practical knowledge—knowing how to play baseball—consists in both practical abilities and also propositional understanding (a point made by Snowdon 2003).

But Stanley and Williamson are not content to leave matters there. When they claim that there is no "fundamental" distinction between knowledge-how and knowledge-that, they mean to insist that propositional knowledge is more basic or fundamental than practical knowledge.

---

she still knew how to do it, only 47 percent answered affirmatively. But second, for reasons indicated in the chapter text, I am doubtful empirical investigation of this sort is warranted. Experiment of this sort gives us data. What we need is insight. This we achieve not by taking data about what people say at face value, for there is no face value to people's words. Context, rhetorical setting, a sense of what is at stake—these are what shape the words we choose, and these are what shape what we say about our choices and understandings. Bengson, Moffett, and Wright's findings do no more than simply kick start the conversation that still needs to be had about what we mean when we say that you (for example) retain knowledge how to ø even when you lose the ability to ø. Ellis's work takes the conversation farther.

They claim that "knowledge-how is simply a species of knowledge-that" (2001). In this they seek actually to defend a kind of intellectualist thesis.

Now, intellectualism is not a doctrine. It is, at best, at attitude. It is Frege's attitude and can be glossed thus: thought and language are autonomous domains; they are formal and are independent of our practical lives, our biology and conscious experience; what makes humans special, what differentiates us from other animals, is our ability to speak, to grasp propositions. And so Stanley and Williamson's claim that practical knowledge is everywhere an achievement of propositional knowledge can be thought of as a kind of vindication of intellectualism.

But Stanley and Williamson fail to vindicate intellectualism. For one thing, advertising to the contrary notwithstanding, they actually allow that *there is* a difference between knowledge-how and knowledge-that; after all what they argue is that to know how to do something is to grasp a proposition, but to grasp it *in a special way.* Moreover, according to their analysis, the difference between knowing how to do something and merely knowing that something is the case has to do precisely with the irreducibly *practical* character of knowledge-how. For they insist that to know how to do something consists in knowledge of a proposition that one has grasped *in an irreducibly practical way.* So at the end of the day, Stanley and Williamson, no less than Ryle, whom they criticize, support the conclusion that to know how to do something is not *merely* to know that something is the case. As for the assertion that the difference between practical and propositional knowledge is not a fundamental one, this would seem to be belied by their own proffered analysis.

Stanley and Williamson end up offering a technical proposal. They show that it is possible to represent knowledge-how constructions as knowledge-that constructions while at the same time doing justice to their ineliminably practical character. What they fail to show is that to do so is to achieve any insight into the nature of practical or propositional knowledge.

As an afterthought: I find myself sorely tempted to say that if either of the two—"know how," "know that"—has a claim to being more basic than the other, it is surely "know how." After all, to grasp a proposition is to exercise one's know-how (one's understanding of words or concepts, say). But it would be a mistake to give in to this temptation. For while it is true that grasping a proposition is something I achieve thanks to what I know how to do, it is also the case that some of what I know in virtue of knowing how to grasp a proposition p is that (say) it is not the case that not-p. The intellectual is practical, yes. But the practical is a sphere for display of the intellect.

Back to the Aesthetic

Disputes about meaning are intersubjectively significant and yet immune to the sorts of "objective" criteria that operate in other areas of our epistemic lives. The criteria are always up for grabs. In this they are like disputes in aesthetics, as Kant understood this domain of inquiry. Aesthetic judgment, Kant insisted, is a matter of feeling. I can't prove to you that something is aesthetically valuable. We are not in the realm of rule-based application of concepts in judgment. And yet aesthetic response is the sort of thing about which it is always intelligible to argue. In contrast with mere expressions of taste, about flavors of ice cream, for example, judgments of the aesthetic value of the work of art happen in a space of criticism. It is always reasonable to ask someone *why* they respond as they do to a work of art; and it is never reasonable to refuse to take that sort of request seriously (however difficult or impossible it may be to explain or justify oneself). An aesthetic judgment is a cognitively rich perceptual accomplishment, even if it is never the sort of thing that can be autonomously justified, proved, or demonstrated. Aesthetics, for Kant, marks a third realm between the objective and the subjective, between the domain of the rule-governed and the domain of mere feeling.

In arguing for the third-realm character of philosophical problems, I have been suggesting that we take what Kant says about aesthetics and generalize it to embrace philosophy. I propose that we acknowledge the fundamentally aesthetic character of philosophical problems themselves (and so, given the interpenetration of philosophy and natural science, the ineliminably third-realm, aesthetic quality of some problems in natural science).[10] Debates about what we mean are not debates about how we feel. They are not debates about "intuitions" (a word that

10. The ideas I express in this paragraph display my debt to Stanley Cavell's essay "On Aesthetic Problems of Modern Philosophy" (1969).

philosophers use too much). But nor are they disputes about the structure of Platonic entities in a third realm. They are not the sort of thing that can be decided by appeal to "recent syntactic theory," or to survey findings, nor by reflections on our neurobiology or evolutionary history. The question, what do we mean when we say "the King's carriage is drawn by four horses" is an opportunity for a kind of stylistic investigation of our intellectual performance. *Are there concepts? Are there home runs?* These in turn are comparable to questions such as *Are there plot twists?* or *Is there épaulement?* The place we look to answer such questions is the work of art, or, in the case of philosophy, our intellectual work and practices themselves.

The aim of philosophical argument about statements of number or the nature of practical knowledge is understanding. We don't seek to uncover practice-independent truths such as: "*really* practical knowledge is a special way of knowing a proposition," or "*really* a statement of number is a statement about a concept." Our aim rather is to get a surview of the whole space of possibilities, of the way the different things that we say, or want to say, or feel we could never say, or deny the intelligibility of saying, hang together. We seek an understanding that consists in finding ourselves, in knowing where we are, and knowing our way about. This has always been the philosophical project. We see this at work in Frege's investigations, and we see it in the work of Socrates.

Afterword

THIS is a book about presence, and its fragility. This is a book about style—about the foundational importance of the idea that we achieve the world for ourselves through different styles of active involvement.

Practices are complicated pageants of habit, autochoreographies of doing and undergoing, acting and accessing. And so are experiences. Style is the face of a practice—it is its perceptible, recognizable quality.

Think of the way architecture organizes what you do. The stairs make it possible for you to go upstairs, but they also control just how you can do this, just where you can go. Architecture enables you to act, but it also disables any number of different ways you might actively have inhabited a place. Architecture freezes you and makes you rigid even as it also opens up a terrain for action.

We see the same dynamic of enabling and disabling (to use Horst Bredekamp's apt language—personal exchange) when we look at pictures, models, language, and other technologies and practices (techniques) of presence. My focus has been on the way these skillful practices open up the world, by affording access. But pictures, models, habits can also hold us captive, as Wittgenstein suggested in *Philosophical Investigations* (1953, §115). Think of the powerful domination of advertising photography. Is there anyone among us who can resist seeing himself or herself, or remaking himself or herself, in the glare of these images? Or, to give a very different kind of example, think of the focusing-power of fMRI images in cognitive science; these seem to require of us that, when we look at these images, we take ourselves to be seeing mind happening in the head, when really, *we* make these pictures precisely to illustrate what we think we know about what is going on inside us.[1]

Can we escape the captivity of our habitual structures, of our language and models and pictures? Can we achieve *new* styles of access to the world all at once? Are we not always inside the old practices, techniques and technologies? How could we ever get outside the spaces carved out by style and habit?

This is where we see once again the importance of presence's very fragile character. It is common to suppose that we live inside paradigms or world views and that from this always-internal perspective we can't even think the outside. There is no outside. There is only inside. And in a way this is right. Our contact with reality is always limited by what we know and can do and so, as we discussed earlier, there is a sense in which we can never have genuinely new experiences.

But what we forget is that the liability to disruption, the porous openness of our ways of doing things to doubts and worries about what is required of us, is as much the hallmark of our practices themselves as is the access to the world they enable. If you can walk, you can trip, and your vulnerability to tripping is not something you forget. The *question of style*—the need for different, maybe better ways of carrying on—is always with us. It arises not at the limits of the framework, but right at home.

Really we need to reject outright the inside/outside, interior/exterior metaphor. A practice is not a space, it is an organization of our habits, and these are slippery, and changeable, subject to different sorts of pressures. Pictures can hold us captive. But our captivity is never total. Which means that this tension between the ways our understanding opens up and the ways it closes off the world for us is a conversation we can't help but keep having. And here's the beautiful thing: the having of the conversation—which, really, is the work of philosophy, and of art—is the very process whereby we remake ourselves and enact new skills and new understandings. And so achieve new styles of contact with the places we find ourselves.

---

1. I discuss this idea—that brain scan images are theoretical models or hypotheses rather than pictures in the ordinary sense—in detail in *Out of Our Heads* (Noë 2010, Chapter 1).

We can't invent new languages or new pictorialities, new ways of thinking. But we also can't stop them from inventing themselves.

This is a book about presence, and the idea that presence is achieved. Consciousness is not something that happens in us, it is something we make. Making requires, in addition to motivation, knowledge and skill, a whole situation in which we happen to find ourselves. It requires something like grace.

Appendix: A List

(from *What We Know Best* by Alva Noë and Nicole Peisl)

You can't see a solid object from all sides at once.
The general form of the work of art is: See me if you can!
You are never alone.
We look in the direction of what interests us.
Loud noise captures attention.
God works in mysterious ways.
There is no art without criticism.
Sounds have no color.
Colors have no pitch.
Choreography has nothing to do with dance.
Home is where the heart is.
There are big dogs and little dogs.
We have what we can reach when we need it.
We think. We feel.
The world shows up for us.
We show up.
Everything has hidden parts.
Down is where the feet are.
I have always been afraid.
Sight is palpation with the eyes.
Architecture is frozen music.
Two Irish men come out of a bar. Yes, this can happen.
There is no such thing as reddish-green.
Every event has a cause.
We are tool users. By nature.

We think with our hands.

Love will keep us together.

The existence of art objects gets in the way of the formulation of clear
    ideas in aesthetics.

Events are creatures of time.

You can't make life in a test tube.

Am Anfang war der Tat.

The time it takes to say "one Mississippi" is one second.

If I say "8," it is 8.

A thought is the sense of a sentence.

It is good to make mistakes in rehearsal.

To say of what is that it is not, or of what is not that it is, is false, while
    to say of what is that it is, and of what is not that it is not, is true.

Form and mass follow function.

Daddy smells like tobacco.

You are always alone.

A person is a dynamic singularity.

Words to memorize, words hypnotize Words make my mouth exercise
    Words all fail the magic prize

The past is present.

The present is past.

You can't put your foot in the same river twice.

Objects persist unperceived.

Today is followed by tomorrow.

Day is followed by night is followed by day is followed by night.
    And so on.

Art is always confusing, at first.

Force is a function of mass times acceleration.

The presence of another person is the most powerful force there is.

We don't decide where to put our feet in the morning.

They will not, no, will not, not now, not ever They will not ever tell
    me who I am.

There is no such thing as a genuinely new experience.

Nimm dir Zeit!

Everything is a lie!

Ornament ist Verbrechen.

No man is an island complete unto itself.

Thou shalt not kill.

I like to see movement.

I am okay.

Don't take shit from no one.

There is nothing to fear but fear itself.

Things fall apart.

Experience is an openness to the world.

Mind and body are and are not distinct.

In times when we thought ourselves indolent, we have discovered that
much was accomplished, and much was begun in us.

What goes up must come down. Spinning wheels go round and round.

We all need someone we can lean on.

Love will get you like a case of anthrax.

Intuitions without concepts are blind; concepts without intuitions are
empty.

Men and women are fundamentally different.

Men and women are fundamentally the same.

A person is not an object.

You can't go home again.

A living being is not a thing.

It is easy to tell the difference between a thing and a living being.

It is easy to tell the difference between a work of art and everything else.

Philosophy is an emotional condition.

I no more wrote than read that book which is the self I am.

We live in a world of arcs, not points.

Life has a beginning, but a work of art always has an introduction.

Don't leave me this way!

We only perceive what we expect to perceive.

I think I love you!

We are at home in the world.

It's easy to write a great song. You just write a song that sounds like a
song you've heard before, but that you haven't heard before.

We assemble reminders.

Time speeds up as you get older.

You need light to see.

We ourselves are dynamically extended world-involving beings.

You don't need light to touch.

What's the best way to catch a fish? Have someone throw it to you!

You are not your brain!

Death is on its way.

The shortest distance between two points is a straight line.

We are empty heads turned toward a single self-evident world!

As a general rule, it is easier to pee than it is to poop.

We are always, already, here.

Language is an instrument.

Consciousness is not something that happens in us. It is
    something we do.

What you see is what you get.

There are no straight lines.

We are one with the world around us.

We achieve presence. It doesn't come for free.

The mind is the sum total of everything we can do.

We live forever!

Music is mysterious.

We love the foods of our childhood.

There is no such thing as a free lunch.

I can't seriously doubt my own existence.

Wer sich schoen fuehlt, ist auch gluecklich.

If you can see that the way ahead is clear, the way ahead will be clear.

I can't seriously doubt your own existence.

The world is everything that is the case.

Life comes to an end; but it has no ending.

I don't have to decide where to put my feet in the morning.

Each of us is trying to find our way to the limits of the known world.

The sun and the stars and the planets revolve around the earth.
    Funny how anyone could doubt this.

All serious discussions end in confusion.

If I could put time in a bottle, the first thing that I'd like to do, is to
    save every day like a treasure and then once again I would spend
    them with you.

Erst kommt das Fressen, dann kommt die Moral.

You can't always get what you want!

It is almost impossible to understand what someone says out of
    context.

The general form of the proposition is: such and such is the case.

The general form of the work of art is: See me if you can!!!

Bibliography

Anscombe, G.E.M. (1959) *An Introduction to Wittgenstein's Tractatus* London: Hutchinson Univ. Library.

Austin, J. L. (1962). *Sense and Sensibilia*. Oxford: Clarendon Press.

Ayer, A. J. (1955). *The Foundations of Empirical Knowledge*. London: Macmillan.

Bengson, J., Moffett, M. A., and Wright, J. (Forthcoming). The folk on knowing how. *Philosophical Studies*.

Bredekamp, H. (2010) *Theorie des Bildakts*. Berlin: Suhrkamp.

Broackes, J. (1992). The autonomy of colour. In D. Charles and K. Lennon (Eds.), *Reduction, Explanation, and Realism* (pp. 421–465). Oxford: Oxford University Press.

Brooks, R. A. (1991). Intelligence without reason. John Mylopoulos, Raymond Reiter In *Proceedings of the 1991 International Joint Conference on Artificial Intelligence* (pp. 569–595). Sydney Australia.

Burge, T. (2003). Perceptual entitlement. *Philosophy and Phenomenological Research*, 67(3): 503–548.

Campbell, J. (2002). *Reference and Consciousness*. Oxford: Oxford University Press.

Campbell, J. (2008). Comment on Noë. *Philosophy and Phenomenological Research*, 76(3): 666–673.

Cavell, S. (1969). Aesthetic problems in modern philosophy. In S. Cavell's *Must We Mean What We Say* (pp. 73–96). Cambridge: Cambridge University Press.

Chalmers, D. J. (2006). Perception and the fall from Eden. In T. S. Gendler and J. Hawthorne (Eds.), *Perceptual Experience* (pp. 49–125). Oxford: Oxford University Press.

Clark, A. (2006). That lonesome whistle: A puzzle for the sensorimotor model of perceptual experience. *Analysis*, 66(1): 22–25.

Deacon, T. (1997). *The Symbolic Species*. New York: W.W. Norton.

Dennett, D. C. (2001). Surprise, surprise [Commentary on O'Regan and Noë]. *Behavioral and Brain Sciences*, 24(5):.

Dennett, D. C. (2002). How could I be wrong? How wrong could I be? *Journal of Consciousness Studies,* 9(5–6): 13–16.

Dreyfus, H. L. (1972/1992). *What Computers Still Can't Do.* Cambridge, MA: MIT Press.

Dreyfus, H. L. (2006). Overcoming the myth of the mental. *Topoi,* 25(1–2): 43–49.

Dreyfus, H. L. (2012). The myth of the pervasiveness of the mental. In J. Schear, *Mind, Reason and Being-in-the-World: The McDowell-Dreyfus Debate.* London Routledge, in press.

Evans, G. (1982). *Varieties of Reference.* Oxford: Oxford University Press.

Fodor, J. A., and Pylyshyn, Z. W. (1981). How direct is visual perception? Some reflections on Gibson's "ecological approach." *Cognition,* 9: 139–196. Reprinted in *Vision and Mind: Selected Readings in the Philosophy of Perception,* pp. 167–228, by A. Noë and E. Thompson, Eds., 2002, Cambridge, MA: MIT Press.

Frege, G. (1884/1978). *The Foundations of Arithmetic* (J. L. Austin, Trans.). Oxford: Blackwell. Frege, G. (1891). Function and concept (P. Geach, Trans.). In Frege's *Collected Papers on Mathematics, Logic and Philosophy,* pp. 137–156, B. McGuinness, Ed., 1984, Oxford: Blackwell. Marginal pagination cited in text above.

Frege, G. (1892). Sense and meaning (M. Black, Trans.). In Frege's *Collected Papers on Mathematics, Logic and Philosophy,* pp. 157–177, B. McGuinness, Ed., 1984, Oxford: Blackwell. Marginal pagination cited in text above.

Frege, G. (1918–1919). Thoughts (P. Geech and R. H. Stoothoff, Trans.). In Frege's *Collected Papers on Mathematics, Logic and Philosophy,* pp. 351–372, B. McGuinness, Ed., 1984, Oxford: Blackwell. Marginal pagination cited in text above.

Frege, G. (1924). Sources of knowledge of mathematics and mathematical natural sciences (P. Long and R. White, Trans.). In *The Frege Reader,* pp. 368–370, M. Beaney, Ed., 1997, Oxford: Blackwell. Marginal pagination cited in text above.

Gibson, J. J. (1979). *The Ecological Approach to Visual Perception.* Hillsdale, NJ: Lawrence Erlbaum.

Gombrich, E. H. (1963). *Meditations on a Hobbyhorse and other Essays on the Theory of Art.* London: Phaidon.

Gumbrecht, H. U. (2004). *The Production of Presence: What Meaning Cannot Convey.* Stanford: Stanford University Press.

Grice, H. P. (1961). The causal theory of perception. In *Proceedings of the Aristotelian Society* (Suppl. Vol. 35), 121–153.

Hayes, A., and Ross, J. (1995). Lines of sight. In R. Gregory, J. Harris, P. Heard, and D. Rose (Eds.), *The Artful Eye* (pp. 339–352). New York: Oxford University Press.

Heidegger, M. (1988). *The Basic Problems of Phenomenology.* Bloomington: Indiana University Press. 1975/1982.

Heidegger, M. (1976). *Logik: Die Frage nach der Wahrheit, Gesamtausgabe* (Band 21). Frankfurt am Main: Vittorio Klostermann.

Hurley, S. L. (2001). Overintellectualizing the mind. *Philosophy and Phenomenological Research,* 43(2): 423–431.

Hurley, S. L., and Noë, A. (2003). Neural plasticity and consciousness. *Biology and Philosophy,* 18: 131–168.

Kelly, S. (2005). The puzzle of temporal experience. In A. Brook and K. Akins (Eds.) Cognition and the Brain: The Philosophy and Neuroscience Movement. Cambridge University Press, New York. 208–238.

Kelly, S. D. (2005). The puzle of temporal experience. In *Cognition and the Brain: The Philosophy and the Neuroscience Movement.* Cambridge: Cambridge University Press.

Kelly, S. D. (2005b). On seeing things in Merleau-Ponty. In T. Carmon and M. Hansen (Eds.), *Cambridge Companion to Merleau-Ponty* (pp. 74–110). Cambridge: Cambridge University Press.

Kelly, S. D. (2008). Content and constancy: phenomenology, psychology and the content of perception. *Philosophy and Phenomenological Research,* 76(3): 682–690.

Kripke, S. (1972/1980). *Naming and Necessity.* Cambridge, MA. Harvard University Press.

Lewis, D. (1980). Veridical hallucination and prosthetic vision. *Australian Journal of Philosophy,* 58: 239–249. Reprinted in *Vision and Mind: Selected Readings in the Philosophy of Perception,* pp. 135–150, by A. Noë and E. Thompson, Eds., 2002, Cambridge, MA: MIT Press.

Lopes, D. M. (2005). *Sight and Sensibility: Evaluating Pictures.* Oxford: Oxford University Press.

Mach, E. (1886/1959). *The Analysis of Sensation.* Trans. by C.M. Williams. New York: Dover.

Margolis, E., and Laurence, S. (2008). Concepts. In E.N. Zalta (Ed.), *The Stanford Encyclopedia of Philosophy* (Fall 2008 ed.). Retrieved from http://plato.stanford.edu/archives/fall2008/entries/concepts/.

Marr, D. (1982). *Vision.* New York: W.H. Freeman and Sons.

Martin, M. G. F. (2004). The limits of self-awareness. *Philosophical Studies,* 120(1–3): 37–89.

Matthen, M. (2005). *Seeing, Doing, Knowing: A Philosophical Theory of Sense Perception.* Oxford: Oxford University Press.

McCandliss, B. D., Cohen, L., and Dehaene, S. (2003). *Trends in Cognitive Sciences,* 7(7): 293–299.

McDowell, J. (1994). *Mind and World.* Cambridge, MA: Harvard University Press.

McDowell, J. (2007a). What myth? *Inquiry,* 50(4): 338–351.

McDowell, J. (2007b). Response to Dreyfus. *Inquiry,* 50(4): 366–370.

Merleau-Ponty, M. (1945/1962). *The Phenomenology of Perception* (C. Smith, Trans.). London: Routledge Press. (French original published 1945)

Milner, D. M ,and Goodale, M. A. (1995). *The Visual Brain in Action.* Oxford: Oxford University Press.

Minsky, M. (1985). *The Society of Mind.* New York: Simon and Schuster.

Nakayama, K., He, Z. J., and Shimojo, S. (1990).Visual surface representation; A Critical Link Between Lower-Level and Higher-Level Vision. In D. N. Osherson et al. (Eds.), *Visual Cognition: Invitation to Cognitive Science* (Rev. ed., pp. 1–70). Cambridge, MA: MIT Press.

Noë, A. (2002). Is the visual world a grand illusion? *Journal of Consciousness Studies,* 9(5/6): 1–12.

Noë, A. (2003). *Causation and Perception: The Puzzle Unravelled. Analysis,* 63(2): 93–100.

Noë, A. (2004). *Action in Perception.* Cambridge, MA: MIT Press.

Noë, A. (2005). *Against Intellectualism.* Analysis 65, 4: 278–290.

Noë, A. (2006). Experience without the head. In T. S. Gendler and J. Hawthorne (Eds.), *Perceptual Experience* (pp. 411–433). Oxford: Oxford University Press.

Noë, A. (2007). Making worlds available [in English and German]. In S. Gehm, P. Huseman, and K. von Wilcke (Eds.), *Knowledge in Motion/Wissen in Bewegung* [TanzScripte series] (pp. 121–127). Bielefeld: Transcript Verlag.

Noë, A. (2010). *Out of Our Heads: Why You Are Not Your Brain and Other Lessons from the Biology of Consciousness.* New York: Farrar, Strauss and Giroux.

Noë, A. (2011). Perception without representation. In N. Gangopadhyay, M. Madary, and F. Spicer (Eds.), *Perception, Action and Consciousness* (pp. 245–256). Oxford University Press.

O'Regan, J. K. (1992). Solving the "real" mysteries of visual perception: The world as an outside memory. *Canadian Journal of Psychology,* 46(3): 461–488.

O'Regan, J. K., and Noë, A. (2001). A sensorimotor approach to vision and visual perception. *Behavioral and Brain Sciences,* 24(5): 939–973.

Peacocke, C. (1983). *Sense and Content.* Oxford: Oxford University Press.

Pinker, S. (1997). *How the Mind Works.* New York: W.W. Norton.

Putnam, H. (1975). The meaning of "meaning." *Minnesota Studies in the Philosophy of Science,* 7: 131–193.

Putnam, H. (1995). *Renewing Philosophy.* Cambridge, MA: Harvard University Press.

Putnam, H. (1999). *The Threefold Cord.* New York: Columbia University Press.

Sartre, J-P. (1940/2004). *The Imaginary.* London: Routledge.

Schear, J. (2011). *Mind, Reason and Being-in-the-World: The McDowell-Dreyfus Debate.* 2012: Taylor and Francis.

Smith, A. D. (2000). *The Problem of Perception*. Cambridge, MA: Harvard University Press.

Snowdon, P. (2003). Knowing how and knowing that: A distinction reconsidered. *Proceedings of the Aristotelian Society* (pp. 1–29).

Stanley, J., (2001). Knowing How. Oxford: Oxford University Press.

Stanley, J., and Williamson, T. (2001). Knowing how. *Journal of Philosophy,* 98(8): 411–444.

Strawson, P. F. (1979). Perception and its objects. In G. F. MacDonald (Ed.), *Perception and Identity: Essays Presented to A. J. Ayer with His Replies* (pp. 41–60). Ithaca, NY: Cornell University Press. Reprinted in *Vision and Mind: Selected Readings in the Philosophy of Perception,* 91–110, by A. Noë and E. Thompson, Eds., 2002, Cambridge, MA: MIT Press.

Tye, Michael (2002). Representationalism and the Transparency of Experience *NOUS* Vol. 36: 137–151.

Ungeleider, L.G. and Mishkin, M. (1982). Two Cortical Visual Systems. In *Analysis of Visual Behavior* eds. Ingle, D.J., Goodale, M.A., and Mansfield, R.J., Cambridge, MA: The MIT Press.

Valvo, A. (1971). *Sight Restoration after Long-Term Blindness: The Problems and Behavior Patterns of Visual Rehabilitation*. New York: American Federation for the Blind.

von Senden, M. (1932/1960). *Space and Sight* (P. Heath, Trans.). London: Methuen.

Wittgenstein, L. (1922). *Tractatus Logico-Philosophicus* (C. K. Ogden, Trans.). London: Routledge and Kegan Paul.

Wittgenstein, L. (1953). *Philosophical Investigations*. 3rd Edition. Ed. and trans. by G.E.M. Anscombe, Oxford: Blackwell.

Wittgenstein, L. (2009). *Philosophical Investigations*. 4th Edition. Ed. and trans. by G.E.M. Anscombe, P.M.S. Hacker and Joachim Schultz. Oxford: Blackwell.

Wollheim, R. (1990). *Painting as an Art*. Princeton, NJ: Princeton University Press.

Acknowledgments

Chapter one was first published in the *Philosophical Quarterly* (2009), 59(236). Chapter three was first published in *Philosophical Topics* (2005), 33(1). Chapter four was first published in *Analysis* (2006), 66(289). Chapter six will be included in Joseph Schear (ed.), *Mind, Reason and Being-in-the-World* (London: Routledge, 2012). Chapter seven was included in John Bengson and Marc Moffett (eds.), *Knowing How: Essays on Knowledge, Mind, and Action* (Oxford: Oxford University Press, 2011).

Index